Date Due

The Gingham Dog

By the same author
Balm in Gilead and Other Plays
The Rimers of Eldritch and Other Plays

The
Gingham
Dog

A play by

Lanford Wilson

Hill & Wang New York

c.17

For
Walt and Violetta
with love and appreciation
(*finally*)

When *The Rimers of Eldritch* was published I sat in front
of the typewriter a long time (days) trying to work on an
"Introduction" for the book. Too many things had
happened that month; the air was waterlogged. At least in
my room. The dedication was all that was left by the time I
finished. I was going to write about Joe Cino. I don't think
I ever will now. He kept appearing in my head saying, "Oh,
come off it."

I once started a poem that began: "What do I owe, and to
whom?" and Marshall Mason remarked: "That promises to
be a long one."

Yeah.

I think of a hundred incidents at once this morning. This
morning after a long useless night of trying to work on
someone's screenplay (screenplay?) I sit at the typewriter

again, wondering whom to credit for the first production of
this play that was written so many years ago and has gone
through so many drafts and hands and productions before it
finally gets committed (sentenced) to print here.

What do I owe and to whom?

Would I hurt the Washington Theatre Club by admitting
that a very good staged reading was presented prior to their
"premiere"? Could I discredit my friends who were in the
reading at the New Dramatists Workshop by admitting
that the first "professional" production of the play was
presented in Washington, D.C.? And wouldn't it look a lot
cleaner just to list the Broadway cast? And what about that
reading at the Clark Center in 1965? And I know it doesn't
make any difference at all; probably none give a damn
really and neither do I.

And there's the matter of dedication. B.H. or E.F., or G.F.
or T.B. or R.L., or pick a letter—probably they had a place
somewhere. Something they said once, something I over-
heard and never even remembered I remembered.

And of course Cino without whom, etc., and is it fortunate
that I can think of him less often—finally. And Ellen and
Michael and Bob. What and to whom? And of course there's
that "What."

What. Well, certainly not just this. Surely not. Later, then.

And to whom? An actress whom I never saw (but lied and
said I did) for whom I wrote the role of Gloria—imagining
the performances as they were related to me by friends,

trying to create a role worthy of those glowing reports. And to Vincent. Later, Vince: I'll get to it. And shouldn't I say something to the exaltation of Broadway reviewers?

No.

And how do you wind through all the wind? (Cubed.)

I suppose I'm so oddly unbitter and so nostalgic only because the play has a longer history than any of the others —from finished script to binding. I've seen three very good very different productions. And so much has happened in between. For one thing, I don't much write like this any more. It should have been obvious to a number of people— but it didn't matter.

The play began with the people—the only place I ever seem to begin. And soon after, the shape. Before it was really begun I knew I wanted the shape to be what it is now. No audience has seen the second act acted much differently from the way I intended it. I thought it was going to be difficult. I suppose it was, but the actors made it look easy. It didn't mean anything to many people. It means a great deal to me.

And what has that big Golden Theatre (which is small) on Broadway (which is on 45th Street) to do with the Caffe Cino? Or the stage of the gym at Ozark High? Actually it wasn't any different. Not a bit. I was working with great people. What came of it? Who knows. I said once somewhere that theatre was in for a big boost—when the Off-Off-Broadway writers and directors began to work in the uptown theatres. I'm not so sure. This year I've seen all the hits. Most all the shows. (Plays, whatever.)

I like *The Gingham Dog* better.

It occurs to me that in its brief run it was seen by more
people than have seen any of my other plays. Now, that
should mean something. It doesn't seem to, but it seems **it**
should.

Who saw it?

Who are we out there in the audience? Today, I mean.

What do we do?

Traveling across the country—meeting people and seeing
places; isn't it unbelievable? It always seems people are
telling us that we have the best damn standard of living in
the world. You know, without checking the statistics, I'll bet
that's a lie. Sweden, Denmark, Holland—looked very
familiar. Looked fine. Germany, England. But it isn't that
we're always bragging or that politicians at the same time
compliment our wealth and credit themselves for it. What
do we do? The young people of my country are alive—they're
living. I don't know how. It isn't just that they are living,
they are refusing to die. While the country dies and dries
and blows away from under them. How do they do it. They
scream in anguish—bitterly angry and desperately sick
because they love this country unbearably; and can't bear it.
We're raping our land. Ignoring (deeply, truly) the Indian,
the black man, and each other. I listen to the opinion of my
country—the voice of the people is reported into my room
on the TV in interviews and how can you keep from crying?
We are wonderful, beautiful, tall, strong, generous, loving,
gentle, kind, concerned, and passionate monsters. What
do we do? Many people believe they are better than other

x

people, *innately;* deserve to keep their wealth, or equal someone's possessions regardless of what it costs—what it costs *them;* their children; and the land. I mean the earth. Dirt. The very soil is dying. The water and wildlife are poisoned and it's like smoking: it's a habit and it's killing us and we know it, but what can we do, we can't stop.

What do I owe and to whom?

(Everybody sing: To the girl who at the age of eight taught me how to copulate imitating her dad's eight-pager that we found in the bottom of the dresser.)

Just for now, at least: (it must be noon, it must be two) I'll list on the next page the three productions chronologically; dedicate the play not to those people from whom I learned it, but to my parents from whom I learned (but did I?) so much more. (It's about time I gave you something.) And for now apologize to Mr. Katz whom I promised (six years ago) to take to the opening of my first Broadway play—I came by the hotel and they said you weren't working there any more. That's all for now. No more apologies.

I don't often start poems and I very seldom finish them and when I do I never much like them. The one about owing and to whom—yes, that would be a long one.

That will be one I never finish.

LANFORD WILSON

July 14, 1969
New York City

THE NEW DRAMATISTS COMMITTEE WORKSHOP
New York City   February 26, 1968

GLORIA   Lea Scott
VINCENT   Michael Warren Powell
ROBERT   David Gallagher
BARBARA   Gretchen Walther

Direction and design by Marshall W. Mason. Stage
Manager, David Rapp. Lighting by Harry Pinkerton.

THE WASHINGTON THEATRE CLUB
Washington, D.C.   September 27, 1968

GLORIA   Micki Grant
VINCENT   Robert Darnell
ROBERT   Bob Spencer
BARBARA   Diane Gardner

Directed by Davey Marlin-Jones. Production design by
James Parker. Lighting by William Eggleston. Production
Stage Manager, Ralph Strait.

JOHN GOLDEN THEATRE
New York City   April 23, 1969

GLORIA   Diana Sands
VINCENT   George Grizzard
ROBERT   Roy London
BARBARA   Karen Grassle

Directed by Alan Schneider. Setting by William Ritman.
Costumes by Theoni V. Aldredge. Lighting by Tharon
Musser. Production Stage Manager, Bruce Hoover. Pro-
duced by Haila Stoddard, Mark Wright, Duane Wilder,
and Harold Scott. Associate Producer, David G. Meyers.

The Gingham Dog

Characters

GLORIA, *a black woman, 27; attractive without being devastating.*

VINCENT, *her husband, 28; strong, handsome. White.*

ROBERT, *a neighbor, about 25.*

BARBARA, VINCENT's *sister, 18; attractive.*

Time

March

ACT ONE: Saturday about noon

ACT TWO: Sunday 5:30 A.M.

The Scene

Gloria and Vincent's apartment on the third floor of a new building in New York's Lower East Side, "East Village." The building is fresh, cold, sterile, hard, and thin-shelled; the walls and ceilings are refrigerator white. Long expanses of flat walls; very sharp, unmolded corners, door frames, etc. Parquet floors. The limitations of the architecture have been rather lovingly overcome by comfortable, tasteful, practical furnishings.

We see the living room, kitchenette, and doors to the hall, bath, and bedroom. A window overlooks the street below. On the long window ledge are rock specimens: quartz crystals, tourmaline, an amethyst geode, etc. Among bracketed hanging bookshelves are components of a rather elaborate stereo outfit. The room also has served as Vincent's studio; there is a drawing board with blueprints spread out over it, a small taboret beside it. The stove, sink, and refrigerator should be practical. The window is open; there are distant noises from the neighborhood.

1

Act One

(At rise, although the apartment is almost compulsively clean, there are piles of clothes in the kitchen, a footlocker beside them; several boxes are packed or ready to be packed and a suitcase is near the door. Gloria is going through a pile of clothes distractedly, dumps them finally, pushes a box aside with her foot, and wanders to the window, a sponge in hand, looking as if to clean without knowing where to start or what to put away. The door is ajar. Gloria is a well-educated, if somewhat vulgar, graduate of New York University. She must have a personal charm, an energy that outweighs a kind of frantic, superficial vulgarity, a detachment from most things, and a driving passion for others. Vincent enters; Gloria does not look around. He comes hustling in, a little winded from the stairs. He is in shirt sleeves, suit pants, a tie slack at his throat. Vincent is a strong, good-looking man, though he looks now, sometimes, rather like a tired young executive. He goes to the drawing board and begins packing whatever chalk, pencils,

etc., that he might want to take. There is a tension between them as though they have been arguing for some time.)

GLORIA
(Lifts a rock from the window ledge, sets it down.)
Do you want this?
VINCENT
(Without looking up.)
What?
GLORIA
This slag glass or rutilated quartz or whatever-the-hell it is.
VINCENT
Is this the mail?
GLORIA
Well, what does it look like?
VINCENT
The mail. Is this all there was?
GLORIA
Uhm.
(There is a mumbling groan characteristic of Gloria, a comic understatement, rather like saying, "I pass.")
VINCENT
Not a damn piece of mail in five days that isn't advertisements.
GLORIA
(Has wandered back to the pile of winter clothes.)
Do you want these in the footlocker?
VINCENT
What are they?
GLORIA
Well, turn your curly head around and see. All these winter clothes. Do you want them sorted or what?

VINCENT
I don't care. Just let them do it when they get here; they're
paid to pack things.
GLORIA
I might want to clear some of this crap off the floor so I can
get started cleaning the place up. Well, I can't do this jazz
alone. Fuck it.
(*Kicks the pile.*)
I said, "Fuck it."
VINCENT
This minute?
GLORIA
Funny.
VINCENT
I don't want any of it. Just throw it all out for all I care.
GLORIA
You'll want "any of it" next winter.
VINCENT
I may not even be in this temperate zone next winter; how
do I know?
GLORIA
What, are you going "on the road"? Vincent the vagrant. A
little late in the spring to start a new life as a boxcar hopper,
don't you think?
VINCENT
"A little late in the spring." That's very good. You're work-
ing at it.
GLORIA
Of course you've hopped everything else. Bandwagons——
VINCENT
You!
(*She nods an acknowledgment and heads toward the book-
cases.*)

7

Now just stay the hell away from the goddamned record player. Just leave it all alone. They'll pack it.

GLORIA

I'm not touching the goddamned Garrard record player. I wouldn't go near it.

VINCENT

O.K., O.K.

GLORIA

Pickering cartridge, Janszen speaker, Telefunken turntable; I wouldn't go near it. It can rot there for all I care.

VINCENT

It won't rot there.

GLORIA

What, are you giving it away?

VINCENT

I am certainly *not* giving it away.

GLORIA

Taking it along with you? In a bag over your back? Hopping boxcars with a pack over your back like Santa Claus, for Christsake. Handing out Deutsche Grammophon records to all the good little kiddies. If they've been real good little mama's helpers, they get *Till Eulenspiegel's Merry Pranks;* only just so-so, maybe *Saint Matthew's Passion, Condensed.*

VINCENT

If you'll be quiet and let me think, I'll get out of your bumbling way. You bumble around the room like a bus.

GLORIA

Are you going to help me take down those shelves or not? Well, never mind, you obviously aren't. I don't know why I asked.

VINCENT

I don't want them. I don't even want them stored. They

never work, they fall off the damn wall. They can be thrown out.

GLORIA

Well, whether you want them or not, they still have to come down.

(*Out of desperation, finally, she settles at the pile of clothes and begins packing them in the footlocker. She folds things, rather than wadding, pressing them with her hand. Even when she is flailing about, you have the feeling that she is packing the trunk neatly.*)

VINCENT

I don't know why you've suddenly decided to move off just because I am. You aren't going to find a better place around here.

GLORIA

Who said I wanted to live around here? You think I'm passionately in love with the Lower East Side? What, have I suddenly got the hots for the electric sitar?

VINCENT

I'd leave all this stuff with you. I don't want it; it would save everyone a lot of headaches.

GLORIA

No, thank you, no. You just store it up; you'll find a use for it. I don't need it, thank you.

VINCENT

Were you here on Thursday?

GLORIA

When was Thursday?

VINCENT

Day before——

GLORIA

No, why?

9

VINCENT

Because I called here——

GLORIA

(*Overlapping.*)

Robert said you called and asked for some of your stuff. I told him I didn't know anything about it——

VINCENT

——It's been right here for five days——

GLORIA

——I don't know anything about it. I haven't looked at it or gone near it——

VINCENT

——You knew what I wanted; you might have been considerate enough to do this one thing; it's not like I——

GLORIA

——It's your work and your blueprints; I told you I'm not interested in it——

VINCENT

It never occurred to you that I wouldn't have called here unless it was impossible.

ROBERT

(*Calling from downstairs.*)

Vincent.

GLORIA

(*With a glance to the open window.*)

It occurred to me that if you were that desperate for them, you could come and get them yourself. You must have managed somehow.

ROBERT

(*Off.*)

Gloria.

VINCENT

Yes, sure, by drawing out the file copy—which has "File

Copy" stamped across them and is strictly against company
policy.

ROBERT

(*Off.*)

Vincent.

GLORIA

(*Moving to the window to look out.*)

I promised to burn the damn things and you don't know
how close I've come.

ROBERT

(*Off.*)

Vincent.

VINCENT

(*As Gloria looks out the window.*)

I don't know what you think that would get you.

ROBERT

(*Off.*)

Hey!

GLORIA

(*Moving back to the kitchen.*)

Someone's calling you.

VINCENT

What the——

(*Looking out the window.*)

It's Robert, looking like a lost duck.

(*Calling.*)

Yeah?

ROBERT

(*Off.*)

You got my other set of keys? I can't find my keys.

GLORIA

What does he——

VINCENT

His keys. Where are Robert's keys? Where——
(*Yelling out.*)
Just hold it a second.

GLORIA

(*Has reached into the cabinet.*)
Here! And you can tell him to keep them.
(*She tosses Vincent the keys.*)

VINCENT

Hey!
(*Soft.*)
Dumb ass, look up. Do you want them or not?
(*He drops them out the window.*)

ROBERT

(*Off.*)
Kill me, why don't you.

VINCENT

(*Moving back to his drawing board.*)
Nut.

GLORIA

When's your sister coming over?

VINCENT

How do I know when she's coming over? She said this morning. She thought she could be of some help.

GLORIA

I'll bet. She could be of some help by staying away.

VINCENT

Please don't start in on Barbara. I know she's useless and you know she's useless, but Barbara at least thinks she's helpful.

GLORIA

I'm hip.

VINCENT

It's no good, really; cleaning the apartment, you know.

GLORIA

Yes, well, I'm going to clean it up if I have to clean around both of you. I don't know why you even came back if you hired movers to do everything for you—just so you could be compulsive all over the living room.

VINCENT

I'm being compulsive? If that's not the pot calling the kettle——

GLORIA

Black.

VINCENT

(*Gloria joins Vincent in speaking the bracketed words.*)
If you clean it up, they'll only say, "What a pretentious [educated nigger]; she only cleaned up her filth to prove [how white she was]." If you leave it dirty, they'll say, ["What would you expect?"] They'll disinfect the place before any kind of tenant will live here, anyway.

GLORIA

Well, they can disinfect all they want. I don't care if they come in here with gasoline and burn out the walls and ceiling. I said it was clean when we moved in and I'll leave it that way.

VINCENT

"*I'll* leave it that way." What a martyr you are.

GLORIA

(*Helping out.*)
. . . *Black* martyr.

VINCENT

What a black martyr you are.

GLORIA

I'll say *we'll* leave it clean when you get off your white ass and help me clean it.

(Robert enters. He is carrying two large sacks of groceries, holding them against his chest, his mail in one hand and the other extending—as much as it can—a brightly colored advertisement. Robert is thin, blond or redheaded, with a kind of haggardly interesting face. He wears glasses and is all angles and rather clumsy. A kind of high voice, nervous and cynical.)

ROBERT

Hey, Gloria—knock knock—you kids want to stop fighting long enough to take this? It was in my box by mistake.

GLORIA

Thanks. You want me to help you?

ROBERT

No, don't touch anything, I got it balanced now. This one's ripped from top to bottom—I think, I can't look. So how's the Master Builder?

VINCENT

Come on, knock it off.

ROBERT

O.K., Jesus. When did you get back?

VINCENT

About half an hour ago or so.

ROBERT

I gotta dump this stuff—I brought you some goodies.

VINCENT

Goodie!

ROBERT

(Exits but continues to yell to them as he takes the groceries to his apartment, directly across the hall.)

So why don't you let a fellow know where you are, for Christsake? I was going to call your office, but it slipped my mind.

VINCENT
(*Yells to him.*)
Thanks.

ROBERT
(*Off.*)
Well, then you called here, so it wasn't necessary. You know you sound like every other Young Man on His Way Up Coming Down From a Six-Day Binge, over the phone? You get those plans all right?

GLORIA
You get those plans all right?

ROBERT
Well, anyway, I just assumed you were out on some really knocked-out trip and would return to earth when you returned to earth.
(*Re-entering with a smaller sack.*)
You get those plans all right?

VINCENT
What plans?

ROBERT
How do I know what plans? The plans you wanted, the blueprints.

VINCENT
We used an office copy.

ROBERT
I mopped you some staples from the café. There's sugar, some tea, and a ten years' supply of mayonnaise.

VINCENT
Tea?

ROBERT
Drinking tea.

VINCENT
Oh.

ROBERT

English Breakfast. Would it were Acapulco Gold, but that's the breaks.

GLORIA

Oh, thanks, I guess ... I don't ...

ROBERT

Take it, it didn't cost me. So how come all the stuff in the car? And don't say, *"What* car?" Your car, downstairs, in front of the building, with all the stuff in it.

VINCENT

I'm leaving, obviously.

ROBERT

For good? I mean that not as opposed to "for bad."

VINCENT

Probably for good. Who knows?

ROBERT

(*Slight pause. Change in tempo. Robert is slightly more serious for a second or two.*)
Well. Condolences, I guess. Really. And here I stand with a welcome home housewarming gift. Well, do we hang the door with black crepe or—sorry, doll—or throw a party or what?

GLORIA

Either one; we won't be here.

ROBERT

It must take a hundred times as much gall to break up as it does to get married.

GLORIA

Don't trouble yourself with it.

ROBERT

(*Overlapping some.*)
Oh, don't tell me, I'm not involved. I only dropped in on my way to work to pick up a few pointers on marriage. I'd

think I might at least close the door; I could hear you all the way downstairs—unless you *want* everyone in the building knowing your affairs, which is possible——

GLORIA

Let them snoop, who cares?

ROBERT

They don't have to snoop, you're drowning out their television sets.

(*To Vincent.*)

So where'd you go on your six-day binge?

VINCENT

Five-day——

ROBERT

Five-day.

VINCENT

Uptown. With friends.

ROBERT

Why, you haven't any friends in the Village? Well, that's easy enough to understand. New suit?

VINCENT

Yes.

ROBERT

That'll teach you to run off without a change of clothes. You're looking very "uptown."

VINCENT

Thanks.

ROBERT

It isn't a compliment, exactly——

VINCENT

I know, I know.

ROBERT

So when are you leaving?

VINCENT

Jesus Christ!

ROBERT

O.K., O.K.

VINCENT

Well, for someone who's not involved!

ROBERT

O.K. I try to be friendly and I'm misunderstood. I should learn. Are we going to see you kids on TV? On *Divorce Court?* I understand you get paid for it now.

GLORIA

No one has said anything at all about divorce; Vince and I aren't discussing it and I don't see any reason for you to.

ROBERT

(*Slowly.*)

Oh. I get it; you're "separating."

(*Pause.*)

That's sort of the opposite of engagement, huh? I'd think you two would have enough balls to just give it up. I mean, you've been fighting for a solid year now that I know of.

GLORIA

Well, that's our problem.

ROBERT

You're telling me.

(*Beat.*)

So what are you doing about your lease?

VINCENT

Gloria might be staying.

GLORIA

No, Gloria is not staying.

(*To Robert.*)

You want a stereo? Vince is giving his stereo away.

VINCENT

No, Vince is not giving it away.

ROBERT

You selling it? How much you want? I might know someone——

VINCENT

No, I'm not selling it.

GLORIA

He's dragging it cross-country.

VINCENT

I'm crating it up with everything else and storing it in
Stephen's basement.

ROBERT

Where you going to be staying?

VINCENT

Uptown. Temporarily, anyway.

ROBERT

With friends. What's her name? You can tell me—almost.

VINCENT

(*Reluctantly, an irritated edge to his voice.*)
The "Y" uptown, probably. It's close to work.

GLORIA

That's convenient.

ROBERT

And they'll let you set up a stereo?

VINCENT

I didn't say I'm taking it along. I said I was storing it somewhere for a week or so, temporarily.

GLORIA

He could set it up there, though; no one would hear much
of anything the way he modulates it.

VINCENT

I do not modulate.

GLORIA

You should let him play a record for you on that precious
Telefunken turntable of his. He sits on top of the amplifier,
practically, adjusting his tracking-force pickup and blowing
on his sapphire stylus. He turns down all the *crescendo* so
it doesn't get too maximum and boosts up the *piano* so it
doesn't get too minimum. *Bolero* starts out on ten and ends
up on one.

VINCENT

I don't own *Bolero*.

GLORIA

And he's a snob to boot.

ROBERT

I'm surprised you're leaving again. I kinna thought you were
back and everything was all right when I heard you fighting
—but then I have this silver-lining view of life. I suppose
it's a communication problem——

VINCENT

A what?

ROBERT

Were you not listening or not understanding?

VINCENT

Either one.

GLORIA

You're right; we speak different languages. It's the fabled
Tower of Babel in a heap right in our own living room.
Rubble. I thought this was only a mess around here—
wadded-up drawing paper and all your old shoes. I thought
I was walking on a cloud of crap. It's not crap. It's rubble.

VINCENT

Right.

GLORIA

Ruins. We couldn't build anything if we worked a hundred
years. Not you and me. You give me a headache.

VINCENT
You give yourself a headache.

ROBERT
Where was the Hutch?

GLORIA
What Hutch?

ROBERT
I don't know, I'm asking you—the place you called the Hutch.

GLORIA
Over on Sixth Avenue; we don't talk about it.

ROBERT
I'd think you would.

VINCENT
It was different.

ROBERT
Haven't you ever wondered how?

GLORIA
(*She looks around. Beat, beat.*)
I thought I'd have a chance to clean this place up before I left; it's going to be great fun with a mob of truckers tearing everything apart.

ROBERT
Very well. You don't talk about it. God, are you nervous.

GLORIA
No, not especially.

ROBERT
You want a Miltown?

GLORIA
Robert, I told you those things aren't any good for you; you don't need them, you just think you do.

ROBERT
Oh, I know, alone in my room I'm perfectly calm, but I

step a foot outside and all my friends are tearing each other apart. . . . Want one?

GLORIA

I said I wasn't nervous.

ROBERT

O.K., you're not nervous. You're tense.

GLORIA

It's going to be great fun with a mob of truckers running in and out of here.

ROBERT

Vince, you want one?

GLORIA

I hope you can decide by now what you want of this stuff or I'm just going to put everything in the footlocker.

VINCENT

Do what you want with it.

ROBERT

You'll understand if I don't offer to help.

GLORIA

That's all right, he's got——

ROBERT

I mean, aside from the fact that I'm not interested in seeing it go, I vaguely remember helping you haul all this stuff up three flights of stairs not that long ago.

VINCENT

You didn't have to help.

ROBERT

When do I ever have anything better to do than meet someone? I'm afraid the year's been considerably better to me than to you, which I hope you understand isn't saying anything.

GLORIA

He's got movers coming half an hour ago.

ROBERT
You'd better get a move on.

VINCENT
Why? I'm not doing any of it. They're going to come and pack it—and wrap it—and lift it—and tote it—and set it up again where I want it when I get a place. I do not intend to——

ROBERT
You know what they'll charge for a job like this?

VINCENT
I don't care. I don't intend to get another hernia carrying all that crap down the stairs. I personally am not lifting so much as a saucer. I'm as sick of all this crap as anyone; I'd as soon chuck it out.

GLORIA
Vincent is discovering he's wasted his youth; he's thinking of a cross-country trek——

VINCENT
I have never said anything about so much as a bus trip to Jersey City. It gets under my skin that we've managed to collect so much crap. Useless, too—possessions. It's "ganglia," dragging me down. It's suffocating. Roots. You know I can't move to another place because if I could take it to Dallas, I wouldn't be living in Dallas, I'd be living here, because I'd be surrounded by the same damn crap that I'd left—or rather, brought along. The same damn stuff.

ROBERT
And the same you in the middle of it. Are you thinking of moving to Dallas?

VINCENT
No.

ROBERT
Just asking.

VINCENT

All this junk. There's no way out of it.

ROBERT

You could give it to the Salvation Army.

VINCENT

Well, what I'm not doing is neatly packing it up into little CARE packages. We brought thirteen boxes——

ROBERT

——Seventeen——

VINCENT

——when we moved in here, with a density unequaled by lead. Gloria could pack the Encyclopaedia Britannica into a shoe box.

(*Pause.*)

And I'm sick of smart-ass labels on boxes: "Some old clothes, and old letters, and the stuff out of that middle drawer, plus three old prophylactics that probably won't work, and the corkscrew."

ROBERT

Do people still use prophylactics?

VINCENT

I don't know.

ROBERT

Mind if I have some coffee?

(*Robert moves to the kitchenette and pours himself a cup of coffee—a habit. He looks rather as if he lives here.*)

About you two; I only got one question. I decided one of you has to be impotent.

GLORIA

What?

ROBERT

I said, one of you has got to be impotent. It's the only way to figure it.

GLORIA

Well, to begin with, how many girls do you know with that problem?

ROBERT

(*To Vincent.*)

Oh. Well, then, it must be you.

GLORIA

Vince is a lot of things, but he isn't impotent—sexually, anyway.

ROBERT

So, sterile then.

VINCENT

Yeah, well, Robert, it's a sad story. I don't like to tell it actually.

ROBERT

(*Sympathetically.*)

Oh, hell.

VINCENT

Yes, you see, I don't talk about it; we try to keep it from people, but I was—well, I was castrated at an early age by a tribe of starving nomad Indians.

ROBERT

Well, that explains it.

VINCENT

You can't really hold it against them—they only did it for food——

ROBERT

Poor devils; but it's sad for you——

VINCENT

Oh, yes——

ROBERT

——being a eunuch like that.

VINCENT

Yes, well, I still like to think of myself as a stallion, Robert.
*(He turns to the drawing board and begins to dismantle it
and the light, etc.)*

GLORIA

Why does one of us have to be sterile?

ROBERT

Well, I guess you don't have to be——

GLORIA

Well, that's a comfort.

ROBERT

But I was telling a friend of mine——

GLORIA

Who's that?

ROBERT

Well, never mind. I have other friends. I have a great many
friends. I have friends I haven't even used yet.

GLORIA

So, O.K.

ROBERT

I was telling him about you two fighting all the time, and
he said, just as a matter of course, "How many——"

VINCENT

I thought you said you weren't involved?

ROBERT

In what?

VINCENT

With marriages breaking up.

ROBERT

Well, *I* may not be interested, but *he* was practically falling
out of his chair. I mean, you don't talk to someone about
what *you're* interested in, you talk about what *they're* interested in. If I talk about my interests, it'd bore him silly.

GLORIA
What are your interests?

ROBERT
And anyway, he said, as a matter of course, "How many children do they have?"

VINCENT
What'd you tell him?

ROBERT
I said, "Six," and he said, "It figures." No, actually, I said, "None," and he said, "How long have they been married?" and I said, "About three years," and he said, "So how come they don't have any kids?" and I said I forget which one of you was sterile. He was very sympathetic.

GLORIA
I'm sure.

ROBERT
Suggested you go to an adoption agency. I told him I'd tell you.

GLORIA
Thanks.

ROBERT
You think about it, though, and he's right. Most colored girls marry a white guy, or vice versa—it's usually vice versa —wonder why that is—someone should run a poll on that— anyway, the first thing they do is start on a whole litter of young. It was the first thing he thought of.

GLORIA
Well, no thanks.

ROBERT
It's all in proving you don't give a damn what people think, see.

VINCENT
Well, maybe we *really* don't give a damn what people think.

ROBERT

Well, it might not be that, but you don't seem to have the normal curiosity. I think they usually have a large family just to see how many different color combinations they can come up with. Like mixing paint.

GLORIA

Maybe we don't have that curiosity.

VINCENT

Gloria's too busy crusading to have that curiosity.

GLORIA

You're damned right!

ROBERT

Don't tell me. I'm about as interested in mixed marriages as I am in mixed vegetables.

GLORIA

It's all right. I'm under fire lately for standing up for what I believe.

VINCENT

Or sitting down, as it were.

ROBERT

Honestly, you take everything so seriously.

GLORIA

Well, it's serious!

ROBERT

O.K., it's important to you.

GLORIA

I didn't say important to me. It's important to everyone alive. I said I take freedom seriously.

ROBERT

When you can get it.
(*Quickly.*)
May it be soon! Jesus. I was only going to suggest, if Vince

could work up some of your concern, go along to a couple of rallies——

VINCENT

Are you kidding? I've got no guilt feelings. You have to be a masochist to be white and go to those rallies lately.

GLORIA

You've got no feelings, period.

VINCENT

(*Still to Robert.*)

When I insult someone, I expect him to leave; and when someone insults me, I leave.

GLORIA

It's those easily insulted puritanical tentacles I admire so. In the history of mankind there hasn't been a more rotten, more disgusting——

(*Overlapping a good deal.*)

VINCENT

You obviously aren't familiar enough with the history of mankind to be——

GLORIA

——The white people have——

VINCENT

——The black people didn't——

GLORIA

——The black people at least——

VINCENT

——The white people did the——

GLORIA

——The black people were——

VINCENT

(*Finally overriding her.*)

——The black people rotted from screwworms in the jungle that they didn't have the sense or intuition to cultivate or build. Just bringing them to a better climate was their first advancement in fifteen thousand years. And *then* you had to be dragged out of the goddamned *trees!*

GLORIA

In the jungle? The black people had empires and temples when you babies were still dirtying up your Alley-Oop underpants! Just don't try to tell me the white man is responsible for one single advancement for the black man. We've had four hundred years of your——

VINCENT

Well, you didn't have enough sense to——

GLORIA

——What one thing—one thing, buddy—can you——

VINCENT

Well, you didn't know anything. My God, we sent you missionaries.

GLORIA

Missionaries?

VINCENT

You didn't know what to *do* with them. You *ate* them!

GLORIA

You're damned right we ate them!

VINCENT

And laws were passed; you sound like nothing——

GLORIA

Laws and laws, your laws and your lawmakers, Old Tom Jefferson with his involuted sentences and calligraphy and his——

VINCENT

Tom Jefferson didn't——

GLORIA

——had slaves on his own Virginny plantation. All men equal—all white men are created equal, maybe——

VINCENT

Screw Tom Jefferson, for Christsake.

GLORIA

You screw Tom Jefferson.

VINCENT

As far as Tom Jefferson was concerned, anyone out of the ruling elite was some kind of schmuck or something——

GLORIA

And you can pass it off as easily as that. Tom Jefferson is a symbol of everything——
(*Robert has looked on—from one to the other—in speechless amazement. Finally he finds his tongue.*)

ROBERT

Hey, hey, hey, hey! What the devil is going on, anyway?
(*Beat. They look at him.*)
Are you really fighting over Thomas Jefferson? Jesus.

GLORIA

Yeah, well, Jefferson drew up the plans and Vince over here is still hammering in the nails.

VINCENT

Gloria's on one of her White Man Is a Cancerous Growth and Shouldn't Exist kicks.

GLORIA

Well, baby, you haven't said anything yet to make me——

VINCENT

If you think hate is as powerful a tool as——

GLORIA

I don't think, remember; I'm just an ignorant jungle flower.

VINCENT

You can say that again.

ROBERT

"The gingham dog and the calico cat, side by side on the

table sat. 'Twas half past twelve and what do you think, not one nor t'other had slept a wink."

(*Barbara enters behind them, smiling and tapping on the door.*)

GLORIA

(*Turning on Robert, overlapping some.*)

Oh, shut up, you shithead!

(*Barbara could be either a very good-looking girl—second best in the class—or a triumph over disadvantages with make-up, dress, and hair style. In either case, she is not really stupid, nor all that naïve, nor all that innocent. She has had a fairly good high school education in Kentucky.*)

BARBARA

The door was open downstairs, so I didn't ring or . . .

(*She has been in New York not long enough to lose the accent—an accent not altogether pleasant, as a Southern accent sometimes is; more nasal, hard.*)

VINCENT

(*After an uncomfortable adjustment.*)

Hello, Barbara.

BARBARA

(*Attempting gaiety.*)

Hi, Vincent, Gloria.

GLORIA

Barbara!

BARBARA

What a charming apartment. I haven't been up here before.

GLORIA

No.

BARBARA

Vince said he was picking up his things and I offered to help . . . anything I can do.

GLORIA

Well, that's damn . . . good of you, Barbara. I'm sure he can use the extra hand.

VINCENT

Robert, uh . . .

ROBERT

I've got to be running. I've got to take these over to the café.

GLORIA

What is it?

ROBERT

Oh, it's locks, door locks. Like for the rest room. We have to keep replacing the locks on the rest-room door. It seems one of the basic laws of behavior is that no man believes someone has beaten him to the john.

VINCENT

(*To Barbara.*)

Robert works for a café—coffeehouse. He's a kitchen boy general janitor.

BARBARA

How do you do?

ROBERT

Pleased to meet you, I'm sure.

BARBARA

You work in a coffeehouse?

VINCENT

He robs them blind.

ROBERT

Cinderella had the pantry; I get the john. Scrubbing graffiti. It's not so bad. You can't get philosophic about it, though, or you're dead—like the writing on the walls—you just have to keep telling yourself it's graffiti. Grrrrr. It's graffiti!

(*Rubs it off.*)

Grrrrr. I wipe it off one week and the next week some joker

33

has put it right back up again. Their art work actually isn't bad at all. A little optimistic, maybe, but not really bad at all, except when it comes to foreshortening——

VINCENT

Robert——

ROBERT

I gotta split; I'll not be long.

BARBARA

Nice meeting you, Bobby.

ROBERT

Bobby. Fine. So long, Gloria—Vincent—Babs.
(*He exits, closing the door behind him.*)

BARBARA

(*To Gloria.*)

I actually didn't know whether you'd be here.

GLORIA

Well, you see, I live here. It's pretty much of a mess right now.
(*Gloria straightens the apartment, almost compulsively.*)

BARBARA

Well, of course, you're packing and everything.

VINCENT

I'm going down now. I have to go next door and get some boxes for the stereo. Damn. I should've asked Robert if he had any.

BARBARA

Who's Robert?

VINCENT

You just met him.

BARBARA

Oh *that* Robert. I don't know as I thought too much of him.

VINCENT

Well, Robert may seem a little fresh at first, but he's a nice noise to have around sometimes—he puts up with a lot of crap.

GLORIA

He puts up with us.

BARBARA

Oh, he seemed nice enough. He's got a sense of humor. I'd just have to get to know him.

GLORIA

He's a good guru.

VINCENT

(*Quickly.*)

Gloria . . . uh . . .

BARBARA

What's a gu——?

VINCENT

I'll bring you back some boxes and you can pack up some books or anything you want. I don't want to take it all.

GLORIA

That's the last thing in the world I want and you know it.

BARBARA

Well, I think you should have it all, Gloria. Isn't that customary?

GLORIA

I don't give a damn what's customary.

BARBARA

But Vincent is the one who works; you shouldn't be expected to——

GLORIA

I work too, or will very shortly.

BARBARA

Well, yes, but——

GLORIA

It was decided before you got here, Barbara; please just stay out, it's settled.

BARBARA

Yes, but it's not right, really, Vincent. What do you want, if anything?

VINCENT

All of it, if that's the way she wants it—everything—every last ash tray.

GLORIA

Good. You bought it.

VINCENT

I didn't necessarily buy it. Who's to say who bought it? Who bought the pepper mill for instance? Who knows?

GLORIA

It was a gift from Hal.

VINCENT

Well——

GLORIA

Please!——

VINCENT

Well, how can you say it's mine?

GLORIA

Take it!

VINCENT

And the bed—you picked it out, bought it—I didn't see it till it was here.

GLORIA

Take it!

VINCENT

I don't know why you have to——

GLORIA

Don't! Don't! Don't do this. Take the bed. Take it all.

Please!

VINCENT

Well, I will.

GLORIA

Well, good.

VINCENT

(*To Barbara.*)

I'm going down to get the boxes. I suppose you can gather up the clothes I have in the closet. And there's a suitcase right there. And the stuff in the medicine cabinet. O.K.?

BARBARA

Fine.

VINCENT

I'll be right back, then.

GLORIA

God damn! Just get gone, Vincent. For godsake just get what you want to take today and just get gone.

VINCENT

Don't worry.

(*He exits, closing the door—not slamming it, but closing it firmly.*)

GLORIA

(*Turns and closes the window. The noise from the street that we have grown quite used to stops abruptly. She sighs and says to herself.*)

Jesus god, I should've taken Robert up on that Miltown.

BARBARA

(*Concentrating too hard.*)

Who's Robert? Oh. Oh yes. What closet are Vincent's things in?

GLORIA

They're not. They're in the suitcase by the door. They have

37

been for three days, if he'd troubled to ask. You can clean out the medicine cabinet if you find anything in it.

BARBARA

Oh. Well, O.K. Where should I put it?

GLORIA

What?

BARBARA

Well, the things . . .

GLORIA

See if there's room in the suitcase, I suppose.

BARBARA

Fine.

GLORIA

Would you mind closing the door, Barbara? I'd like to make a phone call.

BARBARA

Oh, no, not at all.

(*She goes into the bathroom, leaving the door open.*)

GLORIA

(*Dials a number at the phone. To herself.*)

Dumb broad. Deaf, dumb, and blind.

(*Pause.*)

Hello, Rachel? Gloria. Yeah. God, no.

(*The bathroom door shuts. To herself.*)

Dumb bitch. Hum? No, Vince's sister is over—— No, he's here too. Look, baby, what? Is your offer still good? Yeah, he's going to be at some uptown "Y" or something. "Convenient to work." Couldn't you vomit?

(*Pause.*)

Good, it'll only be a couple of days or so, till I can find a place. Well, around; it doesn't have to be much. Swell. No, he's taking the works. I said that from the beginning. Well, you're on the outside; it's different from here. You need anything special? No, probably not till tomorrow. No, it's Sunday. Friday—Saturday—yeah, it's Sunday tomorrow. Thanks, you hear? Well, yeah, but—— Fine. Bye bye.

BARBARA

(Coming out of the bathroom instantly.)

Is this Vincent's razor?

GLORIA

(Looks at her a moment.)

Uh. Yes; it's beat up. I don't know if he wants it.

BARBARA

You never know. And is this your Kings Men or his?

GLORIA

No, I don't think—no, that's Vincent's.

BARBARA

It's almost gone, actually.

GLORIA

Well, you'd best pack it anyway. Your mother gave it to him for Christmas and I'm sure it has sentimental value.

BARBARA

(Sets the suitcase on the sofa, opens it.)

Oh. Well, it must have been some time ago, because I know she hasn't sent him anything in three years. Jesus, his ties are getting all wrinkled.

(Fusses a bit with them, tucks them back. Wandering to the window, wanting to talk.)

What a nice view.

(No reaction.)

Gloria? I know it isn't any of my business . . .

GLORIA

What isn't?

BARBARA

You and Vincent. But I don't understand why you didn't try

39

to work something out. I mean, I know you fight, but you don't fight any worse than anyone else.

GLORIA

Better, usually.

BARBARA

I just really don't know why. You have a lot of friends, don't you?

GLORIA

Uhm.

BARBARA

Well, don't you? Have a lot of friends?

GLORIA

Oh, we have friends by the barrel load. His friends and my friends. Group one and group two.

BARBARA

I just wonder what you'll do.

GLORIA

I've worked, and I like working. Vince didn't want me working, so I quit, and now I can go back.

BARBARA

Did you enjoy it?

GLORIA

Yes. It was interesting, very rewarding work. Yes.

BARBARA

You worked in grade schools—as a social worker, huh?

GLORIA

A psychologist.

BARBARA

That seems so funny, little kids like that talking to a psychiatrist. Do they lie down on a sofa and all?

GLORIA

No, not usually.

40

BARBARA

I don't know why they'd need it, what it'd be for.

GLORIA

For their health. You've heard of antibodies? They're in vaccines you inject into the bloodstream to kill toxins. Well, a child psychologist is a kind of anti-mother.

BARBARA

Do you think Vince has changed much?

(*Pause.*)

'Cause I keep telling him he's changed.

GLORIA

Since when?

BARBARA

I don't know. Since he came up here. . . . Since you've known him?

GLORIA

I don't know. I didn't *see* him the first year I knew him; he had a beard.

BARBARA

A beard?

GLORIA

You knew he had a beard.

BARBARA

When did he?

GLORIA

The whole first year—or nearly—that we were married. It was lighter than his hair. In the sun it was red. Orangish.

BARBARA

He never told us he'd grown a beard.

GLORIA

Well, I guess when he first came up here, he went very native; those Bible Belters usually overdo it a little. And he's stopped playing basketball, so he's getting a paunch. Is that what you mean, changed?

BARBARA

He played ball in New York? Where? I didn't know that.

GLORIA

Across the street from where we lived there were about six basketball courts, and Vince used to be out there every hour he wasn't working. Even when it got cold, they'd be out there.

BARBARA

He still has a practice hoop on the garage door.

GLORIA

Well, he got enough practice here.

BARBARA

He used to be the scrappiest player on our team.

GLORIA

Yeah, well he's pretty scrappy all right. I could look across and keep an eye on him; he was the one with the beard.

BARBARA

Where was that?

GLORIA

Barbara, I haven't got——

BARBARA

No, really, he didn't write or anything, so we didn't——

GLORIA

The first year we were married we had a place up over the Waverly Theatre on Sixth Avenue. A door or two from the theatre. Close enough so when we'd go to bed early, the damn marquee light used to shine in the window. We could've stuck our heads out the window and talked to the man putting up the new bill. And across the street is where they used to play basketball.

BARBARA

Was it nice?

GLORIA

I don't know, Barbara, I didn't play with them.

BARBARA

I mean where you lived?

GLORIA

It was all right, if you happen to like anarchy.

BARBARA

I can't imagine Vince with a beard.

GLORIA

Well he shaved it off quick enough when he went to work uptown. When we were living at the Hutch, he worked with a small company which designed store fronts, and that was hardly what he was looking for.

BARBARA

I don't imagine. What was the Hutch?

GLORIA

(*Closed.*)

Where'd you hear that?

BARBARA

You just said it.

GLORIA

(*She considers a second; then as perfunctorily as possible.*)

That's what they called the place where we lived. One of the black guys Vince played ball with was up from Georgia, used to raise rabbits, and he called the place the Rabbit Hutch because you can't imagine how cramped it got with eight or ten basketball players packed in there eating spaghetti.

BARBARA

(*Sensing Gloria's change and embarrassed by it, doesn't know quite what to say. Awkwardly.*)

43

But then you moved over here. With all this space.

GLORIA

(*Indifferently.*)

Thompson Street for six months and then here. Dragging all this stuff along, both places. Rocks, books, and all. Vince has had them since he was in grade school, I think.

BARBARA

I don't remember them. And then, I suppose you just began ... not seeing eye-to-eye on a few things.

GLORIA

I suppose you could say that.

BARBARA

Like on what?

GLORIA

Name something.

BARBARA

I just wondered if you had thought it out—like **have you** talked at all with your folks, like with your **mother?**

GLORIA

Uhm.

BARBARA

Well, maybe that sounds corny, but I'll bet you haven't, have you? Even being this far away and all, I still write pages to the folks. Every week.

GLORIA

Well, my mother isn't speaking to me lately.

BARBARA

Why not?

GLORIA

She's a segregationist.

BARBARA

Oh. Well, it hadn't hit me like that. Well, I suppose it's natural either way. Mothers and fathers aren't ever pleased with anything their kids do, no matter what, are they? I'll bet she won't be any happier, though, with you separating, will she?

GLORIA

I hadn't really thought about it. I've only talked to Mother about four times since I started school seven years ago, and I doubt if she would have much to say about a separation, either way.

BARBARA

That's terrible. Really it is. I wish you could know the times at home I've defended Vincent. It would surprise you, I'll bet.

GLORIA

I'll bet.

BARBARA

Even before I met you I said if Vincent wants to marry someone of a different race——

GLORIA

Oh god——

BARBARA

——well, then, he knows what he's doing. He'll be a lot happier with her.

GLORIA

You'll look a pretty fool now, won't you?

BARBARA

Oh, I suppose, but they're outside, really.
(*Sitting on the sofa, pulling her legs up cuddly.*)
Do you know what I first——?

GLORIA

Barbara, Barbara, Barbara, before you get all snug and cuddly there—I've got a lot to do and I don't want to be rude, but I just don't feel like a chat. To be perfectly frank, I've never liked you and I can't pretend to——

BARBARA

Oh, I don't blame you, actually. I've known you didn't like me, really. But I've always liked you. A lot. I didn't want to chat or anything. I just——

GLORIA

I just don't care to talk about my private life with you.

BARBARA

I'm not interested in Vincent and your sex life——

GLORIA

Oh, my god——

BARBARA

——Anyway, I'm sure that it was probably just as normal as anyone's. I just wanted you to know that I'm sorry you and Vincent are divorcing like this.

(Gloria looks up sharply.)

I still feel that if you had talked about it, you wouldn't have to be, is all.

GLORIA

Vince and I have spent the whole day *avoiding* talking about it, and I think that's best. The thought of a girl-to-girl chat nauseates me.

BARBARA

(Exiting to the bathroom, quite cool.)

I know why you don't like me—and I don't think it's fair, really.

GLORIA

(To herself, in the second Barbara is gone.)

Phony white tramp.

BARBARA

(Re-entering, a few articles in her hand.)

You feel that I'm Southern. Because I speak the way I do, you feel I'm just a typical Southerner.

GLORIA

Barbara, I don't think of you as typically anything—exactly.

BARBARA

Yes you do, you think I sound like a hillbilly and you're right. I can tell I don't talk as well as you, that I don't sound like people in New York. Are these his?

GLORIA

Yes. Barbara, in you a hillbilly accent is charming. In my brother or one of my sisters it would be a sure sign of stupidity. You can be vapid and dumb and wide-eyed as all hell, but if Cynthia or Nora looked wide-eyed, it would be comical. They have to practically *squint!* It's a joke.

BARBARA

Well, they joke about hillbillies, too. I don't think it's so damn charming. And you're wrong about people laughing at the way Negroes talk. I haven't heard a good colored-people joke in two years. And on TV the only people who can put on a dumb accent any more are Negroes.

GLORIA

Yes, well, we've earned the privilege.

BARBARA

Are Cynthia and Nora the names of your sisters? I didn't know you had more than one sister, Gloria.

GLORIA

I have four sisters and two brothers living.

BARBARA

I didn't know that. How old are they?

GLORIA

I don't know. I haven't seen them in a long time. Cynthia's fourteen; Nora's eight or nine.

BARBARA

Why did you say "living"?

GLORIA

One brother died at birth and a sister died in infancy.

BARBARA

Oh. I didn't know that.

GLORIA

Well, you asked——

BARBARA

I didn't——

GLORIA

——It's an occupational hazard of being a poor Harlem black. You shouldn't trouble yourself with it——

BARBARA

Well, not just black——

GLORIA

——It's something the "outside" shouldn't and doesn't trouble itself with. What did you say?

BARBARA

I said, "not just black." Not just the poor Harlem black. Back home—our home, near Louisville—they aren't city slum or black, they're just poor. But they have baby after baby dying like flies. They have—every shack along the road has a screaming, dirty, skinny mess of kids on the porch and a grave plot alongside the house with four or five markers. It's no different.

GLORIA

It's a great deal different when it's your own sister dead on the bed in front of you, my dear.

BARBARA

You don't think about other people, Gloria; you never once do. And you're very smart, actually, about other things——

GLORIA

When every apartment is wall-to-wall screaming and filth, every pore of the rotting building you live in is death, you don't consider other people's misery, Barbara. I *lived* in misery.

BARBARA

Well, so did millions of other people. *Worse.* Not me, although it wasn't much better. It's not so crowded in Harlem as it is in Indonesia. In Indonesia people, millions of people, are living on just one bowl of——

GLORIA

Fuck Indonesia!

(*Beat.*)

Fuck the Indonesians. What the hell are the Indonesians to me?

BARBARA

Well, I'm not saying you didn't. We sound like a contest of who knows the worst conditions. I didn't want to start something like that. I just came here to help Vincent.

GLORIA

Well, everything is between Vince and me; I didn't intend to go into my dingy family heritage for you.

BARBARA

I didn't know you had a brother and sister that died.

GLORIA

Well, now that you do, I'm sure you won't let it trouble you any.

BARBARA

Of course it will. Maybe I can think that that helps to explain how you feel about——

GLORIA

It doesn't explain anything about me!

BARBARA

It's you're so—I honestly don't know! You tell me all that like you were *proud* of your sister dying and *proud* of——

GLORIA

I Am! Proud! I am proud!
(*Vincent re-enters simultaneously with Gloria's line, carrying the boxes for the turntable and amplifier. Sweetly, simply, in front of Vincent, Barbara replies.*)

BARBARA

Well, then, I don't understand that at all.

GLORIA

(*From Barbara's changed reaction, notices Vincent.*)
Your sister is an imbecile.

BARBARA

(*Peeved.*)
Gloria was telling me how proud she was of her family's lack of—or rather—her—their—her family's poorness, or the family's——

GLORIA

Poverty is the word you're struggling for. She matched me poverty for poverty.

VINCENT

(*Goes to the bookcases; disconnecting the amplifier.*)
Don't fight, children.

BARBARA

Nobody's fighting.

VINCENT

Just sing, "Jesus loves the little children of the world."

GLORIA

I don't know it.

VINCENT

"Red and yellow, black and white."

BARBARA

(*Sings the first few notes of the Sunday school song supersonically high.*)
"Red and yellow, black and . . ."

(*She trails off under Gloria's stare.*)

GLORIA

They sound like jelly beans.

VINCENT

Well, Jesus loves the little jelly beans, too, Gloria.

BARBARA

Can I help? I've just not done anything at all; Gloria had the clothes packed.

VINCENT

Did you?

GLORIA

Thursday.

BARBARA

Gloria has been telling me about her family. It was nice.

GLORIA

Nice?

BARBARA

(*Jumps slightly.*)

Well, I mean that we were getting on so well.

(*She has wandered to the tube of drawings.*)

Is this something from work?

VINCENT

What? Yes. It's just some drawings.

BARBARA

Can I look? I'll put them right back.

(*Takes one out.*)

Oh, it's so complicated. It's not what I thought at all. . . . Is this an apartment building?

GLORIA

It's a crematorium.

BARBARA

A what?

VINCENT

It's a section of an apartment building; put it back **now.**

BARBARA

No, I'm interested; all those little rooms.

GLORIA

Infinitesimal. Well, forget it.

BARBARA

(*Looking up.*)
What?

GLORIA

I said it's the Hanging Gardens of Babylon.

BARBARA

This is marvelous, Vincent.

GLORIA

You tell her to put those up before I remember what I said. Now, I'm not fooling.

VINCENT

Yeah, Sister, roll it up and tuck it back in there, O.K.? You'll get them messed up.

BARBARA

O.K. It's marvelous. How come you got the drawing board at home? Do you have to work much at night?

GLORIA

Oh, yes. They don't measure quality where he works—they weigh it by the pound.

VINCENT

Richter, Richter and Thatcher have a good deal of detail work that I can't get to at the office. I haven't worked much at home lately.

BARBARA

They must be very pleased with you to give you so much to do.

GLORIA

Oh, they just love him to death. Richter, Richter and Trickedher represent his place in society. He's devoted to them—to the exclusion of everything else.

VINCENT

Gloria is a crusader for permanent slums.

GLORIA

That's a lie.

VINCENT

Rather than doing something to help, she talks—about "conditions." Should conditions improve, she'd have nothing to talk about, and talk is all Gloria knows. *Ergo,* Gloria is a crusader for permanent slums.

GLORIA

That's a goddamn lie and you know it. I'd advise you to just quit now.

VINCENT

(*To Barbara.*)

I'm working with a company which is trying to get a contract to build——

GLORIA

(*Overlapping.*)

To build uninhabitable brick ovens. Hi-rise slums. You don't prevent slums or clear them, you *elevate* them thirty stories.

VINCENT

(*Continuing calmly.*)

——which is trying to get a contract to construct a multi-housing unit to replace slum conditions.

GLORIA

Via graft and lobbying and bribery and——

BARBARA

Well, I would think that you'd be very proud of Vincent trying to do good at his job, instead of criticizing him.

GLORIA

Vincent's job has nothing to do with good. Were Vincent's job anything at all good, I would cheer. Vince is trying to do *well* at his job, which is another thing altogether.

BARBARA

Well, I'd think you'd be proud. I know I am. Vince is.

GLORIA

I dunno; Vincent, are you proud?

VINCENT

I think I work as hard as anyone with what I'm allowed to——

GLORIA

But are you *proud?*

VINCENT

I work hard at my job.

GLORIA

But are you proud?

VINCENT

I do what I do well!

GLORIA

You proud, Vince?

VINCENT

Damn hard! Nobody's ever altogether happy with what they're doing, but at least I know that I'll be put on more interesting work as soon as this particular project is over!

BARBARA

(*Slight pause.*)

You are proud, though, aren't you?

54

VINCENT

Yes! I wish I could do more, but I'm proud of the *way* I work, my competence.

GLORIA

His competence at work. The fact that the work they require of him is incompetent totally escapes him. And loyal. To the company.

VINCENT

Yes, my dear, and loyal to the company. Anything else?

GLORIA

Your witness. Barbara?

(*Vincent exits to the bedroom, shutting the door.*)

BARBARA

I just don't see anything to argue about, if you ask me. Vince and I were brought up to believe if you have a job to do, you should do it and do it well. The best you can. Now I just don't know *what* you were brought up to believe——

GLORIA

Well, I haven't time to tell you, Barbara.

BARBARA

(*An edge.*)

You believe in bitching, as near as I can see. Just bitch at everything and everyone, every minute of the livelong night and day, and that's living a good life.

GLORIA

You're closer than you'd think.

BARBARA

I know you claim to be a very religious person, but that's not very darned religious, as far as I can see.

GLORIA

Well, Barbara, there are religions and religions, and we won't discuss how far you can see.

BARBARA

Vince is an architect and if I was you, I'd be very proud of
him.

GLORIA

At best your brother is a draftsman.

BARBARA

(*Yelling; he comes out carrying the clock and a few other
items.*)
Vince! Are you an architect or a draftsman?

VINCENT

It doesn't matter, Barbara. Either one.

BARBARA

What's a draftsman? Is he an engineer? What does he do?

VINCENT

My job is to draw up their specifications—draw plans, blueprints—and also I do a *good deal* of original work of my
own; and I draft the plans for that, as well.

BARBARA

So you're an architect, too.

VINCENT

Yes. I'm an architect. Don't labor it.

GLORIA

Right, absolutely right, and I'm Anna Freud.

VINCENT

I work in a very specialized, a very narrow, qualified, exact-
ing area.

GLORIA

Genocide!

VINCENT

O.K., now, goddammit.

GLORIA

Instant tenement. Add ashes and stir.

VINCENT

We're trying to provide decent housing for people who, quite frankly, don't deserve it. They haven't the sense or ambition to know they live in slums.

GLORIA

Oh they know!

VINCENT

It's good housing, shelter they can afford.

GLORIA

It's a vast brick ghetto, no different from the conditions they live in now, and you know it; and speculating with their lives is evil and you know it, and it's poisoned you.

BARBARA

(*Confused.*)

Who's it for?

GLORIA

For all the starving families in good old Brownsville.

VINCENT

One vast pile of filth. The worst black ghetto in New York, probably. The highest crime rate, the highest childbirth rate, the highest child-death rate, the lowest mentality——

GLORIA

(*Tortured.*)

Right, right, right. Kids' I.Q.'s measured when they're six years old are ten points higher than the same kids measured when they're eleven years old. We used to think that was impossible.

BARBARA

(*Incredulously. She's heard one word in the above.*)

They're *black?* You mean to tell me they're *black?*

GLORIA

As Coley's ass.

BARBARA

They're black and you're against Vincent for trying to help them? You're against that?

VINCENT

Come on now, Barbara, don't get excited.

BARBARA

It was your black sister who died that you were screaming to me about a minute ago. You were screaming about the slums and saying how terribly you lived. You don't want it?

GLORIA

None of us want it.

BARBARA

Well, I guess not. Well, then, don't give it to them. I guess not. It's not good enough, I suppose. I've never heard of anything like it!

VINCENT

Barbara!

BARBARA

No, now. She may think she's bright, but that's just the stupidest thing I've ever heard. That's just the stupidest thing —well, *stick* in your rotting shanties and shake your head about leaving them. And you preaching how your dead sister died because you were poor and filthy and lived in slums.

GLORIA

Barbara, it's no better. It's high and clean and sterile and barren and *does nothing.* Those crummy, cramped, inadequate little apartments. "Units" they call them. It breeds the same thing. You can't elevate the floor, you have to elevate the spirit. It's a vapid gesture, like all the others we've had. Reading the plans for that project is like being given the physical dimensions of hell, and Rancer, Dancer and Prancer are trying to designate that a philanthropic enterprise. And Vince is a loyal and proud part of it.

BARBARA
Is that why you're separating?

GLORIA
No—yes—no. It's enough, but no, not at all. Call it heart failure.

BARBARA
I don't see how it can be bad if it's better. What is the name of the company, Vince?

GLORIA
Maker, Raper and Ditcher.

VINCENT
Richter, Richter and Thatcher.

GLORIA
And if they and all the other companies had their way, all the slums in the world would become a vast sea of sterile, cramped buildings like that. One on top of the other on top of the other. Because there's money in it. Everyone would live in a building like that, in a row of close buildings like that, in a city of buildings like that, in a country of dead buildings like that, like Vince's, in a world of nothing else! Now, would *you* like that?

BARBARA
(*Fast-building exchange*)
It wouldn't be like that.

GLORIA
Would you like that?

VINCENT
Come on.

GLORIA
Living there? Objectively!

BARBARA
Where? I don't know where.

THE GINGHAM DOG

GLORIA

Think for once. Would you like that?

BARBARA

It's only for improvement, isn't it? Of slum areas?

GLORIA

Would you like that? For all whites?

VINCENT

Stop it!

BARBARA

It isn't going to be like that.

GLORIA

Would you like it if it was?

BARBARA

Of course not! No!

GLORIA

Would you like it for you? *Think!*

BARBARA

What?

GLORIA

Units? For you and your family and your kids?

BARBARA

No!

GLORIA

You wouldn't live there?

BARBARA

No!

VINCENT

Come off it!

GLORIA

In Vincent's house?

BARBARA

No, no!

60

GLORIA

Well, neither will I, sister!

BARBARA

(*Continuing almost in one rush.*)

No, no, no. It isn't like that! You hateful bitch, it isn't like that. You're hateful and I'm glad you've broken up, and I knew you would, because at night I *prayed* you would, because you're no different from any other black, and I don't care *who* you try to be like. You're a hateful, vindictive, militant bitch! You think you're smart, but you're *nothing!* And you know it, too. You know you do.

(*Vincent has his arm around her or she would run out. He sits her down on the arm of the sofa.*)

VINCENT

Sit down, it's all right.

GLORIA

I only wanted to show you once that you could think. You don't have to defend it just because Vince is a part of it, and I don't either.

BARBARA

Think! Think! That isn't thinking. I've *never* been talked to like that. By anybody.

GLORIA

You probably——

VINCENT

Knock it off, Gloria.

BARBARA

I'm O.K. now. I just want to know who she thinks she——

VINCENT

No, she's had her little hate purge.

(*To Gloria.*)

Your hate break. Now you can come down.

BARBARA

I'm O.K.

VINCENT

You take these, O.K.?

(*The suitcase, tennis shoes, etc.*)

BARBARA

And go on? Is that all?

VINCENT

I'll bring the rest. You go on. I don't want you around her any more.

BARBARA

O.K.

VINCENT

You can just sit in the car; I'll come down in a minute or two.

BARBARA

You hurry and finish.

VINCENT

Go on.

(*Barbara goes to the door. She opens it, but looks at Gloria for a moment. Gloria looks up, finally.*)

GLORIA

Good-bye, Barbara.

BARBARA

I meant what I said, I want you to know that. . . . I've never liked you, not for a minute.

VINCENT

Barbara!

BARBARA

Vince knows that. I've never been talked to like that. By anybody. Not even by my own father. And I've never liked you.

GLORIA
I never thought you did. The whites taught me duplicity; I know it backwards.

BARBARA
I think you're just like all other Negroes.

GLORIA
Well, I try.

VINCENT
Go on, Barbara.

BARBARA
No, I want to say this. I don't feel sorry for you at all. I'd like to just tear you apart.

GLORIA
But you're too much a lady.

BARBARA
I'm not strong enough or I would try. All you've proved is that you're jealous of Vincent's work, and you don't seem to understand that everyone isn't as shiftless and lazy as you are. I just want to scream, *Yes*, I'm white. Ha, ha, ha. I'm white and you're black and I'm just as happy as hell about it.

VINCENT
(*Firmly.*)
Go on, now, dammit.

BARBARA
I'm sorry, Vincent; I'll see you downstairs. I said I wouldn't say anything, but you can't be friendly with her.
(*She exits.*)

GLORIA
(*Brief pause.*)
That girl is an education. God, you come from an ugly family.

VINCENT

(*Is boiling mad but does not want to show it. He will say anything.*)

I won't be here long to bother you. You better go through those books at least and see what you want.

GLORIA

Box 'em up, I don't want them.

VINCENT

You can't have read them all.

GLORIA

Your benevolence overwhelms me. If I want a book, I'll read it at the library. I'll take my clothes and that's all.

VINCENT

You can have whatever you want. You paid for the bed.

GLORIA

You can say that again. No, thanks. That's all been settled.

VINCENT

Well, I'm not taking the television set. I gave it to you—it was a birthday present. I'm not taking it back.

(*Beat.*)

Where the hell are those movers? I don't know why you had to light in on her.

GLORIA

Who's that?

VINCENT

Barbara. You know who! I don't know what the hell you think you got out of that.

GLORIA

Your sister is an idiot.

VINCENT

Barbara is not a genius, no. She never claimed to be; I've never said she was bright. But there's no reason to attack her. I remembered her as pretty bright when we were living

64

together back home. I was pretty surprised to discover she wasn't. Things can be different from what you remembered. But she's my sister and we used to have some great times at home.

GLORIA

Uhm. I'll bet.

VINCENT

You have a second-class mind.

GLORIA

Well, you have a third-class sister.

VINCENT

I don't know what you think you got out of attacking her.

GLORIA

I think in the back of that mind she might remember that she wouldn't want to live in your house.

VINCENT

And you'll remember she wouldn't want to live in yours.

GLORIA

I can't help the way you people were raised.

VINCENT

She wanted to know why we were separating. She couldn't understand it.

GLORIA

Well, you tell her your story. I don't care what she thinks.

VINCENT

She wasn't that far off in saying it's because you've grown into one callous bitch.

GLORIA

Whatever you want to tell her, just don't practice on me.

VINCENT

She said all along that it wouldn't work; she said so when we were married. My family did and so did yours. We can finally make them both happy.

GLORIA

Who ever thought we'd be the cause of so much happiness?
At least what they won't know is our breaking up didn't
have anything the hell to do with color.

VINCENT

Not directly.

GLORIA

Not directly or indirectly. A thousand things else, maybe.

VINCENT

Indirectly. As a matter of fact, directly. It had to do with the
change in you. And that had only to do with, as you so
delicately put it, with "color." Our separation——

GLORIA

If you'd look at yourself honestly, just once, and ask what——

VINCENT

——Our separation came about because I married an all
right girl who was a bit of a nut and a bit vulgar, and a bit
smart, and in one year she was a goddamned crusader, for
Christsake. She started finding people who—I should say
started *searching* for people—who just couldn't tolerate her.
You hadn't even thought about it before.

GLORIA

Oh, baby, you can't help but think about that and only that
twenty-four hours a day. When you see it all day, you begin
to breathe it and that's all there *is*. Like *air!*

VINCENT

You say that now, but you didn't say it at the Hutch. No,
you might have noticed people eyeing us, looking at us side-
ways, but you never let it bother you——

GLORIA

Yeah?

VINCENT

And after we moved, you took this subtle shift to the way-out left, this red shift to the rear. Any more, you walk down the street, you're not a person, you're a living spring, coiled for counterattack. You joined CORE and SORE and POOR and MORE and God knows what other equal-rights group; every excuse to hate and all you do now is fight. Hate and fight. And fight for what? For freedom, for equal rights, for dignity? For the right to fight, I think——

GLORIA

Right. You're dead right!

VINCENT

I swear to God I don't know what the hell you're fighting for. You used to be a human being, but in the last two years you've become a "black," a professional Negro, and I didn't marry a black.

GLORIA

Like hell you didn't. If you didn't know it, I'm telling you now.

VINCENT

No, sweetheart. The girl I married thought all people were equal, and you—the girl now—you, Gloria—have managed to convince yourself that you're not equal at all. And frankly, I'm inclined to agree with you.

GLORIA

Good. Good. Because equal to you is nothing. Equal to you is subhuman. If you've suddenly noticed you don't consider us your equal, I'm glad you finally realized it.

VINCENT

If I ever had any racist feelings——

GLORIA

Oh, crap——

VINCENT

——then I didn't know about it. But I can't imagine anyone in this world more prejudiced against the Negro than I am

67

now. And two years ago, I swear to God, I didn't feel like that.

GLORIA

Maybe you just hadn't met any.

VINCENT

Well, if that's what it takes, I met a few. I had known people who loved. Lately, you've joined some kind of brotherhood, and it's got nothing to do with love at all. It's so easy, this new-found hate.

GLORIA

New? ... New?

VINCENT

(*Over.*)

It's the easiest thing going. Sister said you were lazy and she hit the nail right on the head. Every damn one of you and your easy, priggy liberals with you——

GLORIA

Not with me, baby!

VINCENT

With you! Crying hate.

GLORIA

Not by a long shot. Janet is my people? Piss she **is.**

VINCENT

It's the easiest thing in the world.

GLORIA

Ronald with that fuzzy blond mop out to *here* is my people?

VINCENT

I know because I found it without even trying.

GLORIA

They may be scared enough to preach equality while their guilt lasts, but, baby, if they're not black, they're not any of them my people, and don't you confuse the two.

VINCENT
Hate, it's right under the first thought. On top of the first thought.

GLORIA
Well, how can you expect anything else, considering the conditions blacks live in today?

VINCENT
How long have they been there? In their ghettos?

GLORIA
You tell me!

VINCENT
And have they had the initiative to organize one rational group, one power, one voice to demand their rights? In any way other than street fights? Riots?

GLORIA
I'm not concerned with your views on the situation.

VINCENT
Vindictiveness?

GLORIA
You just pack and go, and we'll all live easier.

VINCENT
Hate equals hate and it's never netted anything else.

GLORIA
You're learning that, are you?

VINCENT
Yes, I'm learning that!

GLORIA
Well, baby, you walked me up that great white path to security and the Great Society. Taught me how to knuckle under to protect what you thought was your groin, your position—that bulge in your pants is your moneybag.

VINCENT
Aw, for Christsake——

GLORIA

Well, I don't need security, baby, and the boy in the Hutch, may he rest in peace—because he died there—he wouldn't have needed it either. You—whoever you are—can get packed up and go on.

VINCENT

Yeah, he died there and she died there, and why or how the two of *us* ever got together, I can't imagine.

GLORIA

Go on down to your sister.

VINCENT

I got away from Kentucky because people here—I thought, anyway—were open. They could comprehend something outside themselves, respond. They had scope. I wasn't sick of small Southern towns, I was sick of small people—ambitions—hopes—small hopelessness, even. And my friends here were great. I had a place to flop and a place to eat, and I met you and it was wonderful. You probably shocked the hell out of me and I loved it. Because you were freedom to me, Gloria. I'd known people could be free—the way people were meant to live—I just hadn't lived that way. It was great reading Millay and Pound and meeting e. e. cummings in that stupid drugstore every week.* You talking about your kids at school and all their problems. I loved helping you and you seemed to love helping me. Planning for something better for people, sure, but I wanted us to be a part of it, too.

GLORIA

Well, that's always the first mistake.

VINCENT

We can't help everyone else and leave ourselves out. We had

* As cummings died in 1962 each year makes it more difficult for Gloria to be 27 or so and for this meeting to have taken place. In production if it bothers the director, change it to any poet about whom one can feel similarly. I can't.

ACT ONE

a house, the Hutch; it was only a beginning, I wanted to think. . . . Only that.

GLORIA

Yeah, but a beginning of *what,* though? You're not blind, dammit.

VINCENT

You can't live like that forever. You don't have to tell me I died there; you don't know how much. It was great, but I guess it couldn't stand the transplantation.

GLORIA

I guess not. All it comes down to, after all, is——

VINCENT

Is, yeah, I've learned you can live through anything. You can see everything die and come out alive. Empty as a (*a vague gesture, "something"*) but alive.

GLORIA

I'm sure you'll find that when you trot back uptown, some nice, slightly unwashed, white liberalette will cure you of that soon enough.

VINCENT

No, you'll be happy to know that capacity I haven't got. You've done fine.

GLORIA

Oh, she'll cleanse your brown little heart and make it breathe again.

VINCENT

You really don't know—how can I tell you, make you understand, what you've managed to accomplish, what you've done to me?

GLORIA

Just get out. I know what you've become, and I didn't have anything to do with it. A company man, a heartless pile of——

71

VINCENT

After the knifing and twisting of life with you, my capacity
to care for anyone has gone, Gloria. Rotted. Simple radia-
tion poisoning has set in.

GLORIA

You are what you are. A "yes" man.

VINCENT

I will never have the stomach to get near—near another human, living, soul again. I loathe everything I used to admire.
I loathe people for every foul, triple-tongued, political,
hypocritical word they say. I don't hear what anyone says to
me any more, only their motives for saying it. What they
want from me!

GLORIA

Your people maybe—not——

VINCENT

And I loathe your "people" with every grain of strength I
have. After hearing you scream civil rights for three years,
I loathe every group, faction, congregation, complexion,
that ever existed. Automatically.

GLORIA

Well, that's just too——

VINCENT

I used to—back home there weren't many blacks in my town,
but I thought of them as wronged equals. Like the Jews.
We never had a Jew in town and I never knew there was
such a thing as a Jew. And when I moved here and heard the
popular mythology, my heart unquestioningly went out to
another classified people. An oppressed and prejudged people. And then I started meeting friends of mine who talked
endlessly of bargains, who asked what I was making before
what was I doing. They couldn't understand that they were
living and supporting the same image they fought——

GLORIA

You should listen to you sometimes——

VINCENT

——And I kept saying, "It isn't true—the mythology is a lie—it's in me for seeing it. They're no more clannish than Greeks or Chinese or Armenians." And yet all my experience showed me that Simon said, "How much does it cost?" That's what Simon says. "You can buy it for less," Simon says. "What's in it for me?" "Hoard!"——

GLORIA

What do *you* say, Vince?——

VINCENT

——And Rastus says, "Eat shit, baby!" "Get out of the way." "Repay!"——

GLORIA

I don't know your Rastus!——

VINCENT

——"Repay me for the wrong your fathers did my fathers," Rastus says with a madness that comes from years of inborn stupidity and narrow-mindedness——

GLORIA

Rastus is white——

VINCENT

——Rastus says, "Retribution!" I loathe their pompous boasting—their telling you the sexual myth is a sexual myth and then using it as naturally as a fox uses cunning to get what they can of their *petty* desires.

GLORIA

Oh, look around, for——

VINCENT

And, Gloria, goddam you, I loathe you. I loathe the look of you and the oily feel of you and the bitter ear-wax taste, the sour orange-rind smell of you. You disgust me in every

way—your strength and muscle and firm round stomach disgust me, Gloria, and your single-narrow-mindedness. I loathe you because you made me hate. Everything else. And everyone else. You destroy. It's all you know. And you've not got a goddamned thing to rebuild with. Not even hope and not energy and not love. Certainly not love! Not in one of you. For all your popularized warmth! Not even love!
(*He sinks down, drained, sitting on the footlocker.*)

GLORIA

(*She looks at him a moment, then walks a step or two unsteadily to the chair and sits, unrelaxed; with great control, disbelief, barely audible. Finally.*)

I used to pray, I really did, that first year at the Hutch, when I loved you, that we'd have children. I said this . . . when it began, when we had to move up . . . only at first really . . . this could be saved with a child. Like Robert said; a combination half you, half me. And I pictured him—sometimes a boy, sometimes a girl. He was light as you sometimes and dark as me or darker, with all kinds of funny hair problems that I had to contend with. And he was the reason, he was what it all meant . . . and he was always very, very bright. Sometimes dark as chocolate or light as coffee or a beautiful caramel, and as beaming as any of the laughing Spanish kids you see running all over the street. I patterned him after the Spanish kids you see running all over the street. And sometimes he was cinnamon, and when he was, he smelled of cinnamon when I hugged him, and he was always equal parts you and me and that's why I loved him . . . him and . . .

(*Losing control.*)

. . . wanted him. Because he was the love of the Hutch *embodied*. And now the . . . thought . . . the thought of that

child curdles me and I, oh, I, oh Lord, I only thank the benevolent God for being wiser than me——
(*Violently.*)
——because if a son existed now, I swear I'd bash his brains against the goddamned radiator! You used . . . to be . . . and all the while . . . I was saying, Make this white flesh melt into this black . . . and something *new* come from this . . . and saying YES to you. Oh God, it curdles me! And thank God! In his gracious wisdom! And I . . . and I don't care a damn if you loathe me, and if you loathe my people, and I don't give one tinker's damn if you loathe everyone and yourself to boot, and if you've lost your *faith*, and your *heart,* and *hope* and *love* . . .

VINCENT
(*Picks the things up.*)
I'm going . . .

GLORIA
(*Wildly.*)
. . . and your humor, and your goddamned *balls.* I just don't care a goddamn about you. I'll never think of you after this except to thank God in his wisdom for saving me from killing my child! I want a child now, yes, more than ever. And by God, I'll have one . . . with a man . . . a black man like me . . . and my son will be so black he's blue!
(*Vincent goes out the door. She follows him to the door, yelling after him.*)
Black as the night. By God, he'll be *black as the night!*

ROBERT
(*Off.*)
Gloria? Gloria? Gloria, what's wrong?

GLORIA
(*Turning into the apartment.*)
I can't talk——

ROBERT

(*Appearing at the door.*)

What's *wrong? Gloria?* What was he saying to you?

GLORIA

(*Trying to mask hysteria.*)

I'm getting out of here. Nothing. Go on back.

ROBERT

(*Coming into the room.*)

You hurt? Did he hit you? What?

GLORIA

It had to come—his stupid sister here—I'm going back—I am —I know that! Back *home;* I can't take this.

(*She has a small red phone book and is looking through it.*)

I don't even remember their number. I haven't talked to—I haven't even called.

ROBERT

I thought you weren't speaking to them. Or they disowned you or something.

GLORIA

I haven't in two—three—nearly three years. I haven't been home for seven, nearly. But I can't stay on here.

(*Dialing.*)

I was going to stay with Rachel, but I won't; I can't stay down here, I don't care to stay with these *people* down here any longer. Answer!

(*Catching her breath.*)

Oh, God.

(*On the phone, almost without a pause to listen.*)

Hello? Mom? Hello?—— This is Gloria. Is this Cynthia? What?—— Is that you, Nora?—— Little Nora?—— What? This is Gloria, Nora. Is Mama there?—— Nora? I can't hear you, baby, for the noise—— Can you—— Can you turn off the radio, Nora?

(*To Robert.*)
I guess she went to turn it off. Hello? She did.
(*Back to the phone.*)
Hello, Nora. It's been two years—— Honey? I'm coming home, up there—— Where—— What?—— Honey, I can't understand you, baby.
(*Her speech should get slightly Southern, not much.*)
What?—— Speak—— Get farther from the mouthpiece. Where's Mama? At the "market," are you saying? Is she visiting? I'm nervous, baby, I'm sorry—— A neighbor's? What? She's visiting a—— Nora—— NORA! I'm—— I can't understand a word you're saying, baby.

ROBERT

Speak slower.

GLORIA

(*Automatically slower.*)
Where's Mama? What?—— Nora, she's *where?* Ba—ba—baby? She's where?—— WHERE? Say it again—— Nora . . . I'm coming home to live with you. . . . Would you . . . would you like that?—— Would?—— I can't *understand* you! *Speak . . . clearly.* What?—— What?
(*Beginning to be totally incoherent, she can hardly speak, struggling to understand her sister.*)
What?——— No, I *can't* . . . ah, ah, I don't want . . . be . . . so . . .
(*Long pause. She holds the receiver with both hands. Long pause. She hangs up the phone.*)
I . . . can't understand you.
(*Pause.*)
I can't understand a word she was saying. I couldn't understand. What have you done to her? What have you done to *all of them?* Why have—*how could you allow this?*
(*She takes the phone and pulls it, as though ripping it out*

77

*of the wall; the cord pulls from its staples halfway around
the room but remains on the wire.)*

ROBERT

(She isn't facing him. Has totally forgotten him.)
Maybe she was just excited when she heard——

GLORIA

(Whirling.)
Get out of here! Get out of here!

ROBERT

I don't want to upset——

GLORIA

GET OUT! ON! OUT! GO!! GO!!
(Robert exits. She speaks to the phone.)
I can't understand you.
(To no one. To the walls.)
What have you DONE TO THEM?
(Hold a beat. She remains motionless.)

(Curtain.)

Act Two

(Five thirty A.M., Sunday. The apartment is dark except for the blue light from the television facing upstage in the center of the room. The very vaguest light at the window, not enough to shed any light into the room. A warm slit of light under the front door, from the hall.)

(A long pause. The doorbell sounds several times. There is a stirring in the bedroom.)

(All furniture and pictures, curtains, shades, bookcases, everything, have been removed from the room. Dimly on the walls you can see where pictures, etc., have hung. The only things remaining in the room are a few dishes and a pan or two, cups, etc., in the kitchenette area; a table lamp—a new one—near the door, on the floor; and the TV.)

GLORIA
(Offstage, coughs, coming through the bedroom door. She enters the living room, goes into the bathroom. The bath-

room lights go on. Light from the room cuts across the stage. The doorbell sounds again. She is dressed in slippers and a dark violet robe. She should look attractive, though disheveled.)

Son-of-a-bitch! All right now. Son-of-a-bitch.

(She turns on the lamp. Finally buzzes the bell. Sleepy and and very tired. Exhausted.)

(The act should be played very, very slowly. Distantly. Long, wandering pauses. After the first few minutes almost the slightest movement should make a statement.)

(She wanders a few steps from the buzzer. Coughs again, turns off the TV. The bell sounds again; she returns to the buzzer. Holding it down, trying to focus, looking around the room. She does not release the buzzer.)

GLORIA

Christ. Get it? There. Get it?

(Pause, holding it down.)

Think fast.

(Now she releases the button.)

Jesus.

(She walks to the bathroom, shuts the door, goes to the kitchenette, turns on the light, takes a pan, puts on some water. After a moment there is a knuckle rapping at the door.)

Open it, it isn't locked. You've got the damn key.

VINCENT

(Enters. Slowly, doesn't look up. Turning the knob back and forth.)

I think I lost the key.

GLORIA

(Without looking up.)

Or threw it away.

VINCENT

Or something.

(*He fusses a bit with the door latch. Just glancing up.*)

This door is stuck, or something.

GLORIA

You said nine o'clock. It must be five in the morning or after.

(*Both speak in exhausted, drained voices. Whispering.*)

VINCENT

I said about nine.

(*Pause.*)

GLORIA

By no stretch of the imagination is it about nine.

(*Pause.*)

VINCENT

(*Walks around some. They look at each other very little.*)

Man, is this place empty.

(*Brief pause.*)

They get everything packed all right?

GLORIA

They came and I left. I didn't stay to see. I suppose so, it's all gone.

(*Pause.*)

VINCENT

Stephen said it filled his basement. He's a nice guy.

(*Pause.*)

It won't be long. He said you left word you were keeping the bed, which is a good idea. I wanted you to keep . . . you bought it.

(*Pause.*)

There's a lot of other things, actually, that you——

GLORIA

That's all I wanted. I told him to tell you I decided to stay

83

over a few days. I was going to go to Rachel's, and then I was going to go—well, a number of places—but I decided I might stay on here.
(*Pause.*)

VINCENT

You wouldn't find a better place.
(*Pause.*)
It doesn't look like much right now. Anything else you decide you——

GLORIA

I don't think so.
(*Pause.*)

VINCENT

Well, you know ...
(*Pause.*)

GLORIA

I don't think so. I kept some pans, some dishes. Things like that. I'd already packed them; I had to dig around a little.

VINCENT

(*Looking around.*)
The place looks cold, huh? Maybe it's just cold *out*. These sterile buildings, god. Spacious, though.
(*Pause.*)
Who would have thought we had all this space?

GLORIA

Yeah.
(*Pause.*)
You want coffee? I put water on.
(*Brief pause.*)

VINCENT

I suppose.
(*Pause. Gloria makes a cup of instant coffee for him, one for herself.*)

GLORIA

Are you drunk?

VINCENT

Yes. A little. I had a few drinks.

GLORIA

Black or with cream?

VINCENT

Whatta you mean, black or with cream?
(*Beat. She adds cream.*)
Jesus.
(*Beat.*)

GLORIA

There's no sugar.

VINCENT

Christ. Forget it then. Forget it then, that's O.K.

GLORIA

You want powdered sugar? There's powdered sugar.

VINCENT

Fine. Powdered sugar, brown, confectioner's, honey, saccharine, maple syrup if you've got it. I don't care.
(*Pause.*)
Why are we whispering?
(*Clears his throat. In a normal voice.*)
Your neighbors won't know you're home. God that echoes.
Empty room.

GLORIA

Shhhhh. Come on; someone's . . . sleeping.
(*Half-beat.*)

VINCENT

Yeah, well, everyone in the building's—everyone else in
town is asleep. You should see the streets. You'd think
there'd be a few stealthy burglars slipping about.
(*Brief pause.*)

Well, occasionally a wobbly old drunk. Saw a guy trying to walk straight down the sidewalk; he kept listing to the right, you know? Eyes front, walking kinda half-crab, right off the curb, diagonally across the street, and up onto the other sidewalk and into the side of a building before he finally fell over backwards. Still eyes front. Got very excited, like he *knew* that building was going to hit him. Took quite a fall, too.

(*Pause.*)

Well, I figure if a building's got your number on it . . .

(*Pause.*)

GLORIA

Coffee.

(*He takes it off the counter, walks toward the window.*)

VINCENT

Swell.

(*Sips it.*)

God, that's hot.

GLORIA

Shhh.

VINCENT

Is that dawn? Yes, I think that's dawning. Who would have thought it would just go right on? Some nerve the universe, huh?

(*Pause.*)

GLORIA

Yeah.

VINCENT

Who's asleep? What . . . did . . . uh . . . ?

GLORIA

It's a guy. You don't know him.

VINCENT
Sure.
(*Pause.*)

GLORIA
Neither do I, as far as that goes.

VINCENT
But you've *known* him.

GLORIA
No.

VINCENT
Biblically, I mean.
(*Brief pause.*)

GLORIA
That's neither here nor there.

VINCENT
Well, who is he? Let us not be secretive.
(*Beat.*)

GLORIA
It doesn't——

VINCENT
Not that it matters. Outside of simple Kentucky curiosity.
(*Pause.*)

GLORIA
I don't remember his name. He told me. After you left, the movers came and I went out——

VINCENT
For some fresh air.

GLORIA
Because I didn't necessarily care to see the "ganglia" packed and crated and whatever.
(*Beat.*)
And I went to a movie and talked to Rachel for a while, and

we went over to the Surf for the evening and sat and drank, and she left and he came over——

VINCENT

(*With a nod to the bedroom.*)

Him——

GLORIA

He came over and he seemed . . . strong and stupid, and we left and walked this way, and he came up.

(*Beat.*)

VINCENT

For a nightcap. As it were.

(*Pause.*)

GLORIA

Yes.

VINCENT

(*Loudly.*)

Well, and why not? God knows you're on your own.

GLORIA

Don't be loud; I don't necessarily want him to wake up. Besides, he has to get some sleep.

VINCENT

He's resting. I can understand that.

(*Slight pause.*)

GLORIA

He has to get up this morning at six thirty. He didn't get to bed before three. I assume he has to get up, he set the alarm for six thirty. I nearly fainted.

(*Pause.*)

VINCENT

You kept the clock.

GLORIA

I bought one.

VINCENT
You could have had it.
(*Pause.*)
Well, what's he like?

GLORIA
Go wake him up and ask him. What does he *look* like? He's
tall, thin. He is, as nearly as I know, supremely stupid.
(*Beat.*)

VINCENT
Which is a relief.

GLORIA
You'll never know!

VINCENT
Oh, I know!
(*Pause.*)

GLORIA
I don't know what he looks like, just now. I don't remember
his face. He struck me as attractive at the time, I suppose.

VINCENT
Which time was that?
(*Long pause.*)
Well, is he colored, or white, or what?
(*Very long pause.*)

GLORIA
(*She laughs quietly to herself; Vincent joins her without
knowing exactly why.*)
We don't know anything about anyone until we know what
they are. God, you could describe someone down to their
most egocentric characteristic, and you still would have no
idea what they're really like until you know that they're
Irish, for instance—or Scottish. Then you think, "Oh, yeah,
yeah." Got him pegged. Or Greek, or Italian. Suddenly you
know what to expect of them.

VINCENT

Yeah, and?

GLORIA

Well, and nothing, but it makes you wonder. He's Spanish.

VINCENT

This one? Spanish? Jesus.

GLORIA

His principal attraction seemed to be that he didn't speak a word of English. So I say he's stupid; he may be a physicist, for all I know. But I can't understand it, so it sounds stupid. And then he knows the same eight or ten unbelievably profane words in English that I know in Spanish.

VINCENT

Yes, I know them too.

GLORIA

And he used them for terms of endearment, which is a shock, believe me.

(*Pause.*)

So we didn't even try to talk at the bar; we just sat around. It was quite a relief. Smiled a lot.

VINCENT

Yeah. You assume he meant them for terms of endearment.

(*Pause.*)

GLORIA

Why did you come back, Vincent?

(*Pause.*)

VINCENT

I talked to Robert on the phone. It must have rung for ten minutes.

GLORIA

He said. Or rather, he didn't say, he left a note.

(*Pause.*)

VINCENT

God, was he brief. Yes. No. I said, "Are the movers there?"
"Yes." "Are they about through?" "No." "Is Gloria there?"
"No." "How did you get in?" "The movers are here."

GLORIA

Well, I kicked him out. He was getting on my nerves.

VINCENT

What'd you give him back his tea or something?

GLORIA

No.

(Long pause.)

VINCENT

Maybe I should come back some other time. If you're going
to be here, I'll know where to reach you; or I can phone or
something.

(Pause.)

GLORIA

I'd just as soon you didn't, Vince. I'd as soon not see you,
if it's all the same.

VINCENT

Well, goddammit, I can't talk to you with some trick in the
next room, sleeping it off. Whatta you think I am? In my
bed, yet—or your bed—my old bed.

(Pause.)

That sounds like a song.

(Tries a note or two.)

"My old . . ."

(Pause.)

GLORIA

I don't know why you came up here, I told them to say that
I was staying on; I meant if there was anything you had to
see me about. Anything urgent.

(Brief pause.)

VINCENT

I don't suppose there's anything you want to say?
(*Pause.*)

GLORIA

I don't know.
(*Pause.*)
No. I just want to begin something different, something else.
I want to just be able to start out with nothing and see
where I can go this time.

VINCENT

I wondered.

GLORIA

I'm just not up to a post-mortem, I guess. No, I don't have
anything to say . . . no.

VINCENT

(*With some humor.*)
Well, I thought we could shake hands or something and go
away at least not fighting.

GLORIA

(*Some humor.*)
"Don't go away mad"?

VINCENT

I just thought we should say—ah, I don't know. Needless to
say, I've thought about it all evening . . .
(*Pause.*)
They say it's good to have everything out in the open. Well,
that's a lot of horseshit; I—or maybe it isn't. Maybe with the
air cleared . . .
(*Pause.*)
"We have to think about the kids."—"Who's going to sup-
port your mother?" Hell, we don't even have a joint bank
account to settle. I'll have the insurance changed over, or
whatever you have to do to insurance. I'll have my com-

pany's IBM machine contact the insurance company's IBM machine. I guess that's all—it's all been said and done, et cetera.

GLORIA

I'd think so, by now.

VINCENT

Or it hasn't really.

(*Pause.*)

GLORIA

Well, this afternoon for a while I wondered, and I decided we both know what wasn't said—so it's all right to just drop it there.

VINCENT

I suppose. How come you decided to stay on?

(*Long pause.*)

GLORIA

I wasn't going to. I thought for a while that I'd go back uptown. I called Mama—it was only an impulse really.

(*Pause.*)

My youngest sister, Nora, answered the phone and I'm afraid it's been a while. You said you used to think of Barbara as very bright. I used to think Nora was a wonderful, very proper little lady. She's living a mile away in some other country. I couldn't understand a thing she was saying. Not a word. She was trying to tell me Mama was at the store or—I don't know which. I tried to yank the phone out, but it didn't work. It never does.

(*Vincent laughs quietly.*)

Those stupid things never work like they do in the movies. You might know. Anyway, it was upsetting. That's why I went out when your truckers came up. And one of the reasons I didn't want to sleep by myself. José or Prado——

93

VINCENT

Or whatever——

GLORIA

Yeah. Well, people should be able to comfort one another, God knows.

VINCENT

And I suppose he did. Well, that's good.

GLORIA

Not so much; not that it matters.

(*Pause.*)

VINCENT

Oh, well . . .

GLORIA

What?

(*Pause.*)

VINCENT

I don't suppose I'll be back up—or rather down—I don't know that many people down here. I won't have much reason to come downtown.

GLORIA

You'll be busy at work, anyway.

VINCENT

(*A little defensively.*)

Yes. Don't start that. Lay off that, please. Just lay off; I know, I know, but there it is.

(*Pause.*)

GLORIA

(*With humor.*)

Well, for once I wasn't thinking what your work was, just that you'd be busy with it.

VINCENT

Well, *I* was. Thinking about it. Most of the afternoon. I tried to explain to . . .

94

(Falls silent.)

GLORIA

Barbara?

VINCENT

Yes, well, Barbara understands my point of view better than I do. I should have had her explain it to me; I'd have been better off. They—Southerners—have this gimmick, this knack for not understanding something outside of what they accept as right. . . . I don't know, it's this facility they have. You just dial into things that you decide are all right. Everything else doesn't exist. I mean whole countries—whole centuries—don't exist for that girl. Whole problems, if they are problems. It's a facility of the South.

(Pause.)

A human facility, I guess; not just there.

(Pause.)

I got in the room all right. If you can call it a room.

GLORIA

Good. You won't be there long?

VINCENT

No, I'll find a place. That room drives you to finding a place. YMCA. I think they're taking undue advantage of my Christianity. Twenty-four fifty a week for a closet. That's Christian? And you should see it.

GLORIA

Not likely.

VINCENT

(It is much easier to talk about anything else.)

Well, it's something else. You could fit eight of them—ten of them—into this room. They've got some spray paint now that's not one color but about six. Sorta speckledy-spackledy; covers the whole room. Sink, walls, ceiling, floor, bedstead, door—even nails on the wall. Everything. You feel like

95

you're in a time chamber. No up, no down. It doesn't look like paint at all; you know what it looks like? It looks like bird dung. Pigeon droppings. I'm living in a renovated chicken coop. At best you feel that about five painters must have locked themselves in the room, all with a bucket of paint each, and had one hell of a fight.

(*Pause.*)

One window. Looks out onto the air shaft and the tenth floor john.

(*Beat.*)

Which is something else, too, by the way.

(*Pause.*)

GLORIA

But you call it home.

(*Pause.*)

VINCENT

Temporarily.

(*Beat.*)

Everything is scaled down to Wonderland size. Even the soap. You wouldn't believe it.

(*Pause.*)

You open a tiny drawer—which is a very complicated procedure because it's been painted shut—and there's Gideon's Bible. You know something about Gideon? For all his benevolence? He was cheap. You should see that paper he uses.

GLORIA

I'm tired, Vince.

VINCENT

I'll leave; that's O.K.

GLORIA

No, that's all right; I just don't think you came up here to tell me about the "Y."

(*Pause.*)

VINCENT
Well. Yes. I suppose I did, I must have, I can't think of anything else.

GLORIA
What'd you do this evening?

VINCENT
Nothing. Talked to Barbara awhile; she's matriculating in a school for airline stewardesses this spring. I said I thought that suited her perfectly; she was complimented, of course. Talked to Stephen about all the junk in his basement; told him I'd get it out by next week. Saw my room. Left my room and walked around thinking about absolutely nothing. I guess that's something. I was told somewhere that it's impossible to think of nothing, but it isn't. Your mind can go absolutely blank. I assume you had some revelation. You're one up on me if you did.

GLORIA
No. Well, not today. A couple of months ago.

VINCENT
Oh, well, months ago. Months ago I got at least one revelation a day. My daily revelation, I called it. One-a-day revelations.

GLORIA
You said I had or our marriage had stunted your capacity to care any——

VINCENT
Oh, please, don't bring up anything I said this afternoon.

GLORIA
I guess not.

VINCENT
We weren't that far apart, what we wanted.
(*Pause. Uncomfortably.*)

God, there's such—I can't imagine talking to you like this. Like we'd never known each other before. If I'd had known we'd be so goddamned clumsy, I don't think I'd have bothered. Maybe it's that guy in there—I don't think so.
(*Pause.*)
It's a hell of a thing to tell yourself, "Well, fellow, you've made a real hash of your life—or out of three years of it, anyway—maybe your whole life."

GLORIA

I'm hip.

VINCENT

Well, I'll go home.

GLORIA

You want another coffee?
(*Slight pause. He is looking distractedly out the window. It is light enough outside now to cast some light into the room. The room is not dark.*)

VINCENT

Huh? No, I have a taste in my mouth you wouldn't believe.
(*Pause.*)
Well, one more. For the road. Quick one.
(*Pause.*)
I'm glad you're going to stay on.
(*Looks out window. Without much interest.*)
Well, I'll be damned: "Neither sleet nor snow nor dismal dawnings . . ."
(*Pause.*)

GLORIA

(*Looking up.*)
Who is it?

VINCENT

The fabled milkman. Cherrydale Farms. I wonder if cows are really all that goddamned contented.

(*Rubs his fingertips across the sill.*)

Jesus, you cleaned this off; there's a film of dust over it already. What a dirty goddamned city.

(*Holds up his hand. Gloria is across the room at the kitchenette area.*)

Look at that.

(*Pause.*)

GLORIA

It's New Jersey.

VINCENT

(*Looking out the window.*)

He could turn his lights off.

(*Pause.*)

GLORIA

It's late, Vincent. I haven't been to bed yet.

(*She isn't looking at him.*)

(*Pause.*)

VINCENT

(*Still looking out the window, rather delighted by the coincidence.*)

He did.

GLORIA

Good.

VINCENT

The zinc rusted all over the window sill.

GLORIA

Is that what that is?

VINCENT

It's got iron traces in it; probably moisture got to it here and it oxidized. Not much. God, this room looks—oh, well, everything does. Jesus.

GLORIA

You should see it from down there without the drapes.

(*Pause.*)

VINCENT

I imagine.

(*Very long pause.*)

GLORIA

I used to notice windows. I used to walk down streets, like over on Eighth Avenue, where there's a good building and then an old slum building right next to it. And every once in a while some especially dilapidated-looking apartment, grimy as hell, you know, with the old plastic window curtains tied up in a knot and rotting old stained window shades . . . look like maps . . .

Some really Harlemesque apartment. And I'd think, God, that people have to live in places like that. And without really realizing it. Sometimes someone would be leaning out. Or while I was looking up, I'd see, sometimes, just passing by, looking up, someone would pass the window, or lean out, or they'd be moving around up there. And if they happened to be white, I automatically stopped worrying about them. I suddenly lost all empathy—right in the middle of a pain. I didn't dislike them, but right in the middle of my fantasy some old bald-headed Italian in a filthy undershirt would lean out of the window, or some big-busted old mama with her dress pinned up in front, and I'd start thinking about a pair of shoes I wanted to get, or home, or maybe some meeting somewhere.

I didn't really know I did it until I caught myself once. There was a black guy and a white guy, kids playing out somewhere, and I was feeling sorry for the black boy—how he was dressed so poorly. And the other one got up . . . and he had this sore on his head ˙. . .

I don't know; he had blond hair and a sort of bowl cut and his pants leg was ripped up to about his knee—I guess it was—anyway, his knee was all scraped up. And I realized that I was searching the black boy for some injury. Desperately, almost, hoping he'd be *lame* or something.

And I started thinking back and I hadn't always been like that. With the kids at school—but they were such individuals to me. And I tried to help all of them. Probably because I was very happy then, all very secure, when we were living over the theatre there, and nothing much threatened me. (*Vincent laughs, softly, doesn't turn around. She doesn't look up. Pause before she goes on.*)

And I said, Well, baby, we look after ourselves, nobody else does—looks after us—someone had better. I can manage to make that sound humane. But a black who was the least bit sympathetic never escaped me. Beady-eyed, eagle-eyed old Gloria.

And then—it wasn't long ago either, I was—now, God knows, I can take care of myself. You and I know I'll stop and listen to the pitch of any bum; if nothing else, just out of curiosity. It wasn't late at night. Or dark. And I wasn't in a hurry. I don't remember the circumstances, just that I crossed the street.

There was this kind of typical black bum, looking like I was his godmother or something, coming at me: Saint Gloria. Not drunk—visibly—just probably hungry, and for all I know now going to ask me how to get to Columbus Circle or somewhere. Eight feet away from him, I thought: Oh, I just can't take it—I looked both ways, and crossed the street as neatly as you please, never looked back; never gave him a second thought till I was home.

And then I thought, Well, sweetheart, it's spreading. Pretty soon, sister, a crippled little black girl could be pulling at your skirts for old glory, and old Glory'd not even look down.

(*Brushing someone aside disdainfully.*)
Step aside.
(*Pause.*)
You crawled into your company and I crawled into a co-coon. You tucked up into your company and I tucked up into a shell.

VINCENT

Or something.
(*Pause.*)

GLORIA

Yeah, or something.

VINCENT

I should quit working there.

GLORIA

All I was saying, really, is that I've got no room to talk about you. If I took stock of myself, I'd probably find I had no inventory.

VINCENT

It's no way to set up shop.

GLORIA

Uhm. Your coffee's over here growing skin.

VINCENT

Uhm.

GLORIA

(*Toward the window.*)
It's getting morning—if you can call it that. What a dismal goddamn day. I haven't been to sleep yet.

VINCENT

Yeah, me either.

GLORIA

(*Looking out the window.*)
It's just—I *am* a member of a race. A deeply wounded mess of people, and for once somebody—in my lifetime—I know

I'll see the end of an era that suppresses a race. Oh, it's been so incredibly long, and it seems so goddamn impossible; and you see people like Barbara—I don't mean her, but people like her—who have such a strong foundation and don't even know they have it, and you see it in your own people, too—and it all seems so impossible. And you look for a reason, all the time for a reason—because if there isn't any reason, it's just all too goddamn sad or tiring.

VINCENT

Uhm.

(*Beat.*)

GLORIA

Why don't you go up to your room and leave me feeling sorry for myself.

VINCENT

You're not feeling sorry for yourself.

GLORIA

(*A little loud.*)

Don't tell me who the hell I'm feeling sorry for. We didn't used to be callous.

VINCENT

Sure.

GLORIA

(*A little loud.*)

Well, dammit, we didn't.

VINCENT

You're going to wake up your spick trick.

(*Pause.*)

GLORIA

Don't use those words, Vince.

(*Pause.*)

VINCENT

I didn't mean——

GLORIA

I know, but, God—oh, I sound like a schoolteacher; it wasn't his fault he wasn't comforting.

VINCENT

You should get a job; a job is very comforting. You have your job to do. Your niche. And you do your job and guard your niche, and life is very simple. You have only your responsibility—to your company, which is synonymous with yourself, you believe. And any outside responsibility . . . (*Pause.*)
. . . is only a threat.

GLORIA

It wasn't exactly like that.

VINCENT

Even if it was, I don't know how to change now. And *you* believed in a people. "A peoples." That's the trouble; we talk of a group of people as a "peoples." A race—maybe **if** we'd never had the word, we wouldn't have noticed.

GLORIA

Maybe if we'd have been *blind,* we wouldn't have noticed. (*Pause.*)
I wish some goddamn little green people—they're always talking about in the science fiction magazines—would descend from Mars and try to move in on us. Unite this goddamn messed-up country and world in some kind of constructive effort.
(*Pause.*)

VINCENT

(*This exchange all kind of slow, flat, and sad.*)
Poor little green people.

GLORIA

Bastards.

VINCENT
Try to move in.
GLORIA
Green bastards.
VINCENT
Kill our men, rape our women.
GLORIA
Kill our women, rape our men.
VINCENT
Take our jobs.
GLORIA
Try to get into our schools.
VINCENT
We got nothing against race; we got red and black——
GLORIA
"Red and yellow, black and white."
VINCENT
Red and yellow, black and white going to school together, but those little greens are oversexed, stupid—they got pointed heads.
(*Very long pause.*)
GLORIA
Fat chance.
(*Pause.*)
VINCENT
Or something like that.
(*Pause.*)
GLORIA
Poor little greens.
VINCENT
I don't suppose I will quit though; not right now.
GLORIA
Work?

VINCENT

Well, it's experience. Maybe someday I'll tell them what they're doing and they'll fire me.

GLORIA

Then you wouldn't have a job.

VINCENT

How about that?

GLORIA

Don't be poor, Vince; they'd as soon exploit you as anybody. Nobody loves a poor American.

VINCENT

What are you going to do?

GLORIA

I think I'll get on at the Monroe School, I'm pretty sure.

VINCENT

I meant . . .

GLORIA

I can't think about it, it's too draining. It requires all one's energy. That's the only bad thing about it—you can't do anything else. What time is it?

VINCENT

Quarter to six.

GLORIA

Forty-five minutes till the alarm.

VINCENT

I'm fast, too.

GLORIA

Jesus, I'm tired.

(*Very long pause.*)

VINCENT

I wanted us to have children, too. I had the same picture of him that you did, actually.

GLORIA

Well, what we don't want is to talk about private little things like that. Warming little intimacies aren't for us.

VINCENT

No.

GLORIA

I don't want to feel that maybe there's something there when I know there isn't.

VINCENT

No. Still . . .

GLORIA

I'd like to just—wipe it off altogether.

VINCENT

Sure.

GLORIA

Maybe for you and maybe for me, but not for us. Not any more. We've spent three arduous years finding that out.

VINCENT

Two years.

GLORIA

I'll buy that; the first year we didn't learn a thing.

VINCENT

(*With humor.*)

Maybe we learned everything the first year and forgot it the next two. Then we started getting principles—they take a lot of maintenance. It wasn't the same. When I think back, I can't believe it.

GLORIA

Uhm.

VINCENT

Well, keep in touch.

(*Very long pause. She shakes her head finally, slowly.*)

GLORIA

I really don't see any reason.

(*Pause.*)

VINCENT

Well, whatever you want, either way.

GLORIA

(*A bit more energy.*)

I mean, if I get run down by a truck, they'll contact you—
you've got my insurance policy.

VINCENT

(*Laughs.*)

I'll get it changed. There's time for all that jazz. Well, I'm
sober now, anyway.

GLORIA

(*A bit more energy.*)

I want to get an apartment started, get some things in here,
I guess.

VINCENT

I have to get a place, too.

GLORIA

Sometimes I think this place will be fine, and sometimes I
want to move into a very small furnished room. If I wasn't
totally ingrown already, now would be an ideal time to re-
tire into myself.

(*Vincent laughs, just softly.*)

VINCENT

I'll go on; you know where to reach me.

GLORIA

You keep saying I know where; I don't know why.

VINCENT

Well, if something comes up.

(*Long pause. He finishes the coffee in a gulp.*)

God, that's cold as a bitch.

GLORIA

I'm glad you came **by.**

VINCENT

I'm sober now, anyway.

GLORIA

Do you have to go to work?

VINCENT

It's Sunday.

GLORIA

Right, right. Get some sleep.

VINCENT

You too. Crawl in with your hot pepper in there.

GLORIA

Well, it seemed like a good idea.

VINCENT

I'm glad I came over; I didn't know I was going to really; I was in the Village, wandering around. Habit, I suppose.

GLORIA

(*Smiles.*)

Uhm.

(*Pause.*)

I'm glad you came back; it's better this way. I guess.

VINCENT

I'm sober now, anyway.

(*He touches her arm briefly.*)

Well, I'll see you. Or I won't see you, as it were. I wish you luck.

GLORIA

You, too, Vincent.

VINCENT

(*Rapidly, briskly now.*)

Oh, well, Jesus Christ; good-bye, good luck, and God bless, I guess. O.K.?

GLORIA
(*Walking him to the door.*)
O.K. Good-bye to you; good luck, Vince.
(*Vincent stands beside her at the open door for a moment, then exits briskly. Gloria closes the door.*)
Poor little greens.

(*Goes to the stove. Lights a cigarette. Turns off the overhead light. Puts the two cups into the sink. Runs a little water. Turns off the lamp by the door. The room is quite light now. A very gray morning dim-light slants into the room. She looks at the front door. Looks to the bedroom door. Pauses. Wanders to the window, looking out into the street. Takes a drag of the cigarette.*)

(*Crosses her arms. Leans against the window sill. The only movement in the room is the smoke from Gloria's cigarette. Silence.*)

(*A full thirty-second pause, please. Nothing moves. Gloria continues looking blankly out the window.*)

(*Curtain.*)